SOCIALIST EDUCATION IN KOREA

Selected Works of Kim Il-Sung

SOCIALIST EDUCATION IN KOREA

Selected Works of Kim Il-Sung

Edited by
Riley Seungyoon Park
Cambria York

Foreword by
Derek R. Ford
Curry Malott

Afterword by
Derek R. Ford

Published by *Iskra Books* 2022

All rights reserved.
The moral rights of the editors, contributors, and author have been asserted.

Iskra Books
Madison, Wisconsin
U.S. | U.K. | Ireland | Canada | Australia | India
Iskra Books is the imprint of the *Center for Communist Studies*, an international research center dedicated to the advancement of academic and public scholarship in the fields of applied communist theory and Marxist-Leninist studies.
ISBN-13: 978-1-0880-0548-4

British Library Cataloguing in Publication Data
A catalogue record for this book is available from the British Library.

Library of Congress Cataloguing-in-Publication Data
A catalog record for this book is available from the Library of Congress.

Art, Design, and Typesetting by Ben Stahnke
Printed and Distributed by IngramSpark

CONTENTS

Editor's Preface
Riley Seungyoon Park..1

Foreword
Contextualizing the *Theses on Socialist Education*: Lessons for Revolutionary Pedagogy Today
Derek R. Ford and Curry Malott...4

1. On Eliminating Dogmatism and Formalism and Establishing *Juche* in Our Ideological Work
Kim Il-Sung...27

2. On Publishing the Theses on Socialist Education
Kim Il-Sung...55

3. The Theses on Socialist Education
Kim Il-Sung...64

4. On the Full Implementation of the Theses on Socialist Education
Kim Il-Sung...114

Afterword
Chongryon: The Struggle of Koreans in Japan
Derek R. Ford..138

Kim Il-Sung (15 April 1912 - 8 July 1994), born *Kim Song-Ju*, was a prominent guerrilla leader, revolutionary, and theorist who played a foundational role in the establishment and leadership of the revolutionary state of the *Democratic People's Republic of Korea*, serving as its beloved Premier until his death in 1994—the longest serving non-royal head of state in the 20th century.

EDITOR'S PREFACE

Riley Seungyoon Park

June 25, 2022 will mark the 72nd anniversary of the "official" start of the Korean War. Since then, there have been many changes in the geopolitical landscape and the world order, which has since become unipolar with the onslaught of U.S. imperialism. The United States has continued its military occupation of the southern regions of the Korean peninsula and has placed brutal economic sanctions onto the Democratic People's Republic of Korea (DPRK, or north Korea). In the closing of the 2010s and the opening of the 2020s, the U.S. has turned its attention towards the People's Republic of China, doing whatever it can to isolate and delegitimize the advances and successes that the PRC has accomplished since its 1949 revolution as well as the successed and advances made by the DPRK following its 1948 inception. In an effort to encircle and isolate the PRC, the US has set up bases in Okinawa, Hawai'i, and south Korea—using these outposts to exercise military support for its own geopolitical and financial interests. The US occupation in the region remains the primary obstacle to Korean reunification.

Like many young Koreans living in the belly of the beast, I was constantly exposed to the U.S. propaganda machine.

Growing up in school, we were constantly told that the Korean War started with the north invading the south and that the U.S. was a benevolent protector for South Korea. This, coupled with the US imperialist wars in Afghanistan and Iraq, made me believe that the U.S. was "protecting" "freedom and democracy." It wasn't until I was halfway through my undergraduate studies that I began to look more critically towards the propaganda machine and pull back the veneer of the falsifications that had been instilled in me at a very young age. Thus my political education had begun and it was a foundational period in making me the communist I am today.

Throughout my political education, I was returning to my roots and learning the true history of Korea and the U.S. occupation. This led me to the works of Kim Il-Sung and his applications of Marxism-Leninism as it applied to the conditions of the DPRK. I was amazed by the building of a socialist society after the overthrow of the Japanese colonial empire, and the strength of building towards internationalism as a point of solidarity with all oppressed and colonized people. I was so impressed at how DPRK built relationships with the Palestinian national liberation struggle, the anti-apartheid struggle in South Africa, and the anti-colonial revolutions in Africa, Vietnam and South America. I learned of how the DPRK built solidarity with the Black Panther Party and connected the struggle for Black liberation to the Korean struggle against U.S. imperialism, with Kim Il-Sung describing it as "our common enemy."

The stories of the communist revolutionaries both here and abroad inspired me to organize for a world free of exploitation, and for liberation. I dreamt of a liberated and reunified Korea, free from the iron grip of the American empire; I dreamt of the proletarian revolution in the belly of the beast.

With all of this said, it is such an honor and a privilege to present to you *Socialist Education in Korea: Selected Works of Kim Il-Sung*. I dedicate this preface to all colonized and oppressed peoples around the world who fight for a better world and future. I dedicate this to my comrades and siblings in Korea who fight for a free and united Korea.

Toojeng!

FOREWORD

Derek R. Ford and Curry Malott

CONTEXTUALIZING THE *THESES ON SOCIALIST EDUCATION*: LESSONS FOR REVOLUTIONARY PEDAGOGY TODAY

Publishing the selected works of Kim Il-Sung on education might be a controversial move in the United States, especially within academia, where even the most critical of scholars almost unquestionably accept the position of the country that they otherwise critique. The very fact that it is controversial is, as we will see, one reason for the need to deepen and spread a proper understanding of Korean history and the Korean struggle for socialism, independence, and reunification. Why, after all, shouldn't educators in the U.S. study the educational projects undertaken in other countries? Why are some—like Finland—acceptable, while others—like the Democratic People's Republic of Korea (DPRK, or north Korea), unacceptable?[1]

On what grounds would it be deemed controversial? In fact, there's almost a proportional relationship between the demonization of the DPRK and the level of ignorance one has about the state, the country, its government, its people and Party, and

---

1 In this book, we have chosen to refrain from capitalizing "north" and "south" Korea to acknowledge the forced division of the peninsula by U.S. occupation into two separate entities. - *Editors' note.*

its history. This is particularly striking given the recent interest in "decolonial" and anti-colonial education, socialist and communist educational methods, and socialism and communism more generally.[2] Given these recent activist and scholarly interests, we think it's appropriate for a work like this to appear. This book not only provides key insights into the socialist educational project in Korea—including its pedagogical philosophies and practices, organizations, purposes, government institutions, and more—but it also helps to provide a more accurate description of the DPRK's socialist project as articulated by the state's founder and, for almost five decades, central leader. Reflecting on the ongoing implementation of the *Theses on Socialist Education* six years after their official implementation, Kim Il-Sung summarized the ethos of the *Theses* as one of intellectualizing and revolutionizing all elements of society.

JUCHE AND KOREAN LIBERATION

While the mainstream media and bourgeois politicians in the U.S. portray the DPRK as an unpredictable, irrational, and ultimately unknowable entity, there is not only a general consistency in the decisions of the state and the ruling party (The Workers' Party of Korea), but also a consistent ideological reference: *Juche*. In fact, even a cursory investigation into any aspect of the DPRK—whether it be military affairs, foreign policy, education, or culture—will result in coming across the foundational concept of *Juche*.

Juche is predominantly translated into English as "self-reliance" or "independence," but a more accurate and comprehensive translation is "subjecthood." *Juche* was first articulated by

---

2 See, for example, Vijay Prashad, *Red Star Over the Third World* (London: Pluto Press, 2019); Ariella Aïsha Azoulay, *Potential History: Unlearning Imperialism* (New York: Verso, 2019); Jodi Dean, *Comrade: An Essay on Political Belonging* (New York: Verso, 2019).

Kim Il-Sung in a now famous speech included as the first chapter in this book, although its origins—like those of the DPRK itself—are found in the anti-Japanese guerrilla struggle. In particular, the founding of *Juche* is located in a speech Kim Il-Sung gave in June 1930 at a meeting of the Young Communist League and Anti-Imperialist Youth League in Kalun, a city in Jilin Province, although it wasn't explicitly articulated until a few decades later.

Jilin Province is located in Northeast China, in Manchuria, and shares a border with north Korea. Jilin is important in the history of the Korean struggle for several reasons. It's the place where Kim Il-Sung joined the resistance movement, and also where, as a teenager, he founded the Down-With-Imperialism Union, which contemporary literature in north Korea considers as the original foundations of the Workers' Party of Korea (WPK). A large number of Koreans had fled to Jilin to escape the brutal Japanese colonial occupation of Korea, and Jilin was home to the largest base of the Korean resistance.

In the struggle against Japanese imperialism, Korean and Chinese communists (and, at various points, nationalists) were part of a united front. In fact, at the urging of the Third International (Comintern), which at the time was organizing the world communist movement, Korean communists joined the Chinese Communist Party. It's estimated that, when the merging process was consolidated in 1931, as much as 90 percent of the Chinese Communist Party (CCP) was actually Korean, as their efforts at recruitment among the peasants in the region had been much more successful.

The formation of a united front was a complicated task, and one which had a profound influence on the *Juche* idea. Kim Il-Sung and the revolutionary leadership had to win the masses over from the bourgeois nationalists, who wanted to appeal to capitalist powers or solely on the Third International to bypass the struggle required for independence, which included the "movement for cultivating national strength through education and industrial development."³ The Korean communists under Kim Il-Sung's leadership also had to deal with social democrats and ultra-leftist theories and leaders, which he saw as dogmatic and inappropriate to the current conjuncture. The ultra-leftist theories were those that merely mapped on tactics and strategies developed elsewhere onto the Korean context, and the social-democratic theories were those that insisted on building socialism without establishing a proletarian dictatorship.

The problem with the bourgeois nationalists, the social democrats, and the ultra-leftists emanated from "the peculiarities of the development of Korean history, characterized by worship of great powers."⁴ Not only were elements looking to the Soviet Union and China, but others even endorsed U.S. president Woodrow Wilson's doctrine on the self-determination of nations.

In response to those who wanted to build the anti-colonial struggle and the future independent Korea by relying on outside forces or self-styled leaders parroting theories from elsewhere, Kim Il-Sung formulated the slogan "The people are my God," which encapsulates "the spirit of approaching everything with the masses of the people at the centre and boundlessly treasuring them." As Kim Jong-Il recounts, Kim Il-Sung "clarified the truth that a revolution should be carried out not by anyone's approval or instruction but by one's own conviction and on one's own responsibility that all problems arising in the revolution should be solved in an independent and creative way."⁵

---

3   Editorial Board, *History of Revolutionary Activities of President Kim Il Sung* (Pyongyang: Foreign Languages Publishing House, 2012), 17.

4   Ibid., 19.

5   Kim Jong-Il, *On the Juche Philosophy* (Pyongyang: Foreign Languages Publishing House, 2002), 24.

The Partition of Korea and the Charting of an Independent Socialist Path

After decades of arduous and complicated ideological and armed struggle, the defeat of Japan was imminent by the summer of 1945. As the Korean revolutionaries were sweeping down the peninsula rapidly, the U.S. proposed that Korea be temporarily divided at the 38th parallel, with the Soviets taking control of the north and the U.S. taking control of the south. The Soviet Union accepted this proposal. Having suffered catastrophic losses in their war against the Nazi regime, the Soviet Union was in desperate need of respite, and made several concessions to imperialism in response to this need. Under the agreement, both the U.S. and the Soviets were to withdraw troops from their respective territories in 1948. The Soviet Union did, but U.S. troops continue to occupy the south.

Although the imperialist narrative is that the Soviets installed a "puppet" regime, the real power in the north rested in the 70 people's committees set up by people in the north–complemented by 145 people's committees in the south. Thus, the U.S. proposed the division of the peninsula because it understood that the entirety of Korea would be under the people's communist control if it didn't militarily occupy the south.

While the Soviet Union set up a civil apparatus in the north, its primary function was to provide the legislative apparatus through which decisions made by the people's committees could be greenlit. These people's committees, which were locally organized, would consolidate with other socialist and revolutionary organizations to form the WPK in June 1949, knowing that they needed a unified revolutionary party in power with broad bases in the masses.

The U.S. war against Korea, which lasted from June 1950 until July 1953 has ultimately ended. The U.S. was forced to sign an armistice agreement after they had been unable to make any gains above the 38th parallel. The north, however, was decimated in the war, having suffered years of carpet-bombing, massacres, and the use of chemical and biological weapons. The rebuilding of the country was an urgent and monumental task. At the same time, it's likely that the socialist Koreans signed the armistice as a result of pressure from the USSR and PRC. Internal debates also occurred within the WPK about how best to develop the country along socialist lines, and also about where the DPRK should stand in relation to the developing Sino-Soviet split.

Stalin died in 1953, and after an internal struggle in the Communist Party of the Soviet Union, Nikita Khrushchev emerged as First Secretary in 1955/1956. Reactionary forces leapt on this instability in Poland and Hungary in the anti-Soviet revolts which arose and were eventually defeated. At the same time, differences between the USSR and the People's Republic of China were simmering. What began as a struggle over particular policies developed into an ideological and political state-to-state struggle.

The struggle between the PRC and USSR became so intense that in 1960 the Khrushchev leadership recalled all Soviet technicians, engineers, and advisers who were, at the time, playing a critical role in China's economic development projects.

Ultimately, however, the north Koreans needed assistance and cooperation from both the USSR and PRC, but the state and people didn't want to be dictated to by either of these socialist giants in a *quid pro quo* arrangement for aid and trade.

The divisions within the international communist movement came to a head in 1956. In February of that year, Khrushchev made his "secret speech," in which he repudiated Stalin and his legacy. In April, the USSR sent a delegation led by Leonid Brezhnev to the WPK's Third Party Congress. In his address, Brezhnev agitated against "cult of personality" issues in the DPRK. While Kim Il-Sung was visiting the USSR over the summer, the pro-Soviet faction and the pro-PRC Yonan faction conspired to depose his leadership at the upcoming plenary session of the

Central Committee.

This intra-WPK struggle was not taking place only behind closed doors, however, but was actually fought out in public. For example, on August 1, 1956, the official newspaper of the Central Committee of the WPK, *Rodung Sinmum*, ran a column endorsing all Soviet criticisms of the Stalin era, including the "cult of personality." This was clearly a direct, public attack on Kim Il-Sung from within the top leadership. At the plenary session that began August 30, leaders of both factions attacked Kim, arguing that the state and party apparatuses should be headed by separate leaders. They also attacked him over the path of economic development. Under Kim's Il-Sung's leadership, the state and Party at the time emphasized heavy industry and military development while also prioritizing light industry and agriculture. Importantly, which we'll explore more below, Kim's "economic policy increasingly emphasized mass mobilization appealing to people's patriotism, and the fundamental task of installing socialist consciousness in the masses through ideological education."[6] Kim's opponents, however, argued that the country should focus on consumer goods, and should therefore rely on the USSR and PRC for heavy industry.

During their speeches, both factions were shouted down by the rest of the Central Committee. Almost all of the leaders of both factions were expelled from the WPK.

In Kim Il-Sung's words, the crisis in the international communist movement came to a head in 1956-57 and "the world imperialists and international reactionaries, availing themselves of it, unfolded an extensive 'anticommunist campaign.'"[7] U.S. impe-

---

6   Moe Taylor, "Between Market Socialism and the New Man: Cuban and north Korean Economic Discourse in the 1960s," *North Korean Review* 17, no. 1 (2021): 13.

7   Kim Il-Sung, *Juche! The Speeches and Writings of Kim Il-Sung*, ed. Li Yuk-Sa (New York: Grossman Publishers, 1972), 27.

rialists stepped up aggression as "anti-Party revisionist elements within the Party came out to attack the Party, taking advantage of the complicated situation and with the backing of outside forces. The anti-Party elements within the Party and their supporters abroad, revisionists and big-power chauvinists joined forces in opposition to our Party and carried out conspiratorial activities to overthrow the leadership of our Party and government."[8] There were internal factions within each of these elements: "Nationalists divided themselves in different groups and got engrossed in bickering, turning to big powers, instead of thinking of struggling by drawing on the forces of the popular masses."[9]

By making *Juche* official policy, the WPK and state apparatuses fastened the country's direction around "the principle of solving for oneself all the problems of the revolution and construction in conformity with the actual conditions of one's country, mainly by one's own efforts."[10] *Juche* was formulated against "dogmatism and flunkeyism towards great powers" as a dynamic doctrine organized around "independence in politics, self-sustenance in the economy, and self-defense in national defense."[11]

Education was a central component in the production of comrades who looked to outside forces. Although the new socialist government immediately prioritized education according to the *Juche* idea, they nonetheless had to send students to foreign countries to learn technical and scientific skills. "Those who had studied abroad as well as those who had returned home from abroad preferred foreign things to ours, trying to copy foreign

---

8   Ibid., 28.

9   Kim Il-Sung, "On the Korean People's Struggle to Apply the Juche Idea," in Kim Il-Sung, *Answers to the Questions Raised by Foreign Journalists* (Pyongyang: Foreign Languages Publishing House, 1991), 41.

10 Ibid., 45.

11 Ibid., 46.

things mechanically."[12]

The importation of foreign ideas was not merely of an ideological or political nature, but of a cultural nature as well. That is to say, some in the WPK were looking to the USSR and PCR not only for economic support, but also for cultural support. Some were arguing, for example, that Koreans should adopt Soviet dressing styles or Chinese artistic styles. Because Korea is a nation with thousands of years of history, and a nation which was (and is) still colonized in the south, the opposition's portrayal of Korean culture as "backwards" or somehow inadequate repelled many in the DPRK's leadership and population.

Juche was thus 1. born out of the anti-colonial struggle, 2. forged through the experience of forming a united front, 3. sharpened in response to different factions within the party that ultimately rejected the *Juche* approach to development, and 4. implemented to mobilize the Party and people to forge an independent path that would secure their state from efforts by the much larger socialist countries—who were both valuable allies—to impose their own agenda on the DPRK. The mobilization of *Juche* allows for endless tactical flexibility in foreign, economic, and social policy even today.

Looking back from 2022, it's indisputable that the *Juche* political ideology has been successful. The Koreans played a key role in defeating Japanese imperialism, forced the U.S. to sign an armistice in 1953, and survived the Cold War, the opening up of China, the dissolution of the Soviet Union, and the overthrow and collapse of the European Socialist Bloc countries. While navigating these endlessly complex geopolitical challenges, they've managed to rebuild their country from rubble. *Even the CIA* admitted that the DPRK includes "compassionate care for children in general and war orphans in particular; 'radical change' in the position of women [and no prostitution]; genu-

---

12   Ibid., 45.

inely free housing, free health care, and preventative medicine; and infant mortalitiy and life expectancy rates comparable to the most advanced countries until the recent [early 1990s] famine."[13] This doesn't include other accomplishments, such as the genuinely free educational system, which includes daycare and goes from preschool to the highest levels of academia.

SOCIALIST EDUCATION

The particular characteristics of socialist education that would be developed in the north stem from a need created during Japan's colonial reign between 1910 and 1945. For example, under Japan's rule, Korean culture and political independence was viciously repressed, as the Korean language and political organizations were outlawed. Koreans were even forced to adopt Japanese names.[14] In the remedial forms of education that existed during the colonial period a curriculum that glorified all things Japanese, including Japan's imperial flag, dominated.

The super exploitation, dispossession, and extreme violence that accompanied Japanese colonialism was justified by biological and cultural racism. This bigotry audaciously portrayed Koreans as lazy, unsanitary, untrustworthy, immoral, and unstable. So-called "bad" Koreans were portrayed as making it difficult for "good" law-abiding, virtuous Koreans. Socialist education has to counter the destructiveness of Japanese propaganda that continues to be perpetuated by Japanese and U.S. imperialism in their ongoing efforts to overthrow the people's self-determination in the northern half of the peninsula.

The communists in Korea, while part of the broader class struggle and working at different times—and in different capac-

---

13   Cited in Bruce Cumings, *North Korea: Another Country* (New York: The New Press, 2004), iii-ix.

14   See Ken C. Kawashima, *The Proletarian Gamble: Korean Workers in Interwar Japan* (Durham: Duke University Press, 2009).

ities—with their comrades in the Soviet Union and what would become the People's Republic of China, were from the beginning untethered to the theoretical dictates of either grouping. This is one way in which the *Juche* idea can be traced back much further than the 1955 speech. When the time came to engage in the reconstruction of the country after the devastation of the U.S. war, there was no doubt that the country needed to build—and rebuild—its heavy industry. Yet this was no mere economistic formula. On the contrary, as indicated earlier, it was predicated upon the promotion of socialist consciousness in the north. In other words, the material and ideological foundations of communism had to be built, and here we see Kim Il-Sung emphasizing that "it is the ideological one that is most important to conquer." This is because the construction of new material foundations depended upon the enthusiasm of the masses, which in turn was predicated on their understanding of communism.

Immediately after the liberation of the north from Japan, the WPK set out to correct the lack of indigenous cadres to build their socialist society and, to pursue this task, Kim Il-Sung told a Delegation of the American Popular Revolutionary Alliance of Peru that they "set up a university before anything else in the teeth of every hardship [...] We did not waver in the least," he says, and they "brought in teachers and intellectuals from all over the country, some of the intellectuals even from the southern half of Korea."[15] Already by the time of the writing of the *Theses*, the Korean government established a universal eleven-year compulsory education system and several prestigious universities that trained intellectuals, technicians, artists, professors, and more. He himself had already enacted a *Juche* approach to education at the very beginnings of the anti-colonial struggle when he formed the Down-With-Imperialism Union. "Some of my

---

15   Kim Il-Sung, *On the Korean People's Struggle to Apply the Juche Idea*, (Pyongyang: Foreign Languages Publishing House, 1983), 39.

comrades," he reported, "advised me to go to Moscow and study at the university funded by the Communist International."[16] He understands why they wanted him to do so, as that was the premiere international school in revolutionary leadership, organization, and struggle. But Kim Il-Sung disagreed, "thinking that it would be better to learn while struggling among the people than studying in Moscow. Our people, not people at Moscow or Shanghai, were my teachers."[17]

The philosophy underlying the educational program is the belief in the masses to make their own history through, specifically, their *independent* and *inventive* ideas and actions. Kim Il-Sung spoke of this as making *Juche* the principle and guiding force of pedagogy, insofar as revolutionary education "is creative work to develop the people who live and act in specific conditions." "We must solve all the problems of theory and practice that arise in education," he continues, "creatively by our own efforts in accordance with the situation in our country and in the interests of the Korean revolution."[18] This was a well-rounded curriculum encompassing communist theory as well as the natural and social sciences, artistic practices and aesthetic theories, culture, and more.

Such an expansive curriculum would require international help and the guidance and assistance of comrades in other socialist states. Yet, in accordance with *Juche*, none of this should be accepted uncritically or universally. The importation of scientific education, for example, was done not programatically but in a way that adopted it to the unique Korean conjuncture. This, in turn, meant the rejection of subsuming Korean education and development to any other major power, a subsumption that

---

16   Ibid., 43.

17   Ibid.

18   Kim Il-Sung, *Theses on Socialist Education* (Pyongyang: Foreign Languages Publishing House), 8.

would, in effect, amount to the very dogmatism urged against in the 1955 speech.

The method of approaching such foreign knowledge and educational practices through the *Juche* philosophy was, Kim Il-Sung formulated, through imbuing revolutionary education with revolutionary practice. "Theory for theory's sake and knowledge for knowledge's sake that are detached from revolutionary practice are utterly useless in our society," he writes. The beginning point of education are our concrete practices, which then compel the production of theories to understand those practices. Then, such theories are used to recontextualize the concrete practices out of which they emerged. Such praxis, however, can't be formulated sporadically across the country but has to achieve some level of uniformity. This is one reason why the socialist state has to take responsibility for education:

> Only by educating all members of society continually can any differences in the ideological, technical and cultural standards of people be eliminated and the aim of making our whole society working-class, revolutionary and intellectual be achieved.[19]

Another reason why education must be organized through the socialist state is precisely to produce a new revolutionary collectivity by unlearning the individualistic conceptions of people and society propagated by colonialism and capitalism.

One way in which this educational praxis takes place is through students actively participating in the production of their towns and cities. As Helen-Louise Hunter notes, beginning in middle and high school, university and college students engage in volunteer labor as part of their studies, even constructing the road connecting Kaesong and Sinuiju. Much of the work takes place in the evening which, she says, "has a certain excitement for teenagers. Students enjoy seeing friends whom they have not seen for a while. There is a sense of camaraderie and esprit de

---

19   Ibid., 11..

corps as they work together through the night."²⁰ Students are active agents in constructing and reconstructing their own built environment and, through doing so, experience the communist collectivity that works to overcome the individualism of capitalist imperialism. They do this by participating in youth organizations, including the Children's Union, the League of Socialist Working Youth, and others.

Beyond formal schooling, education in the DPRK continues through participation in Party and state organizations. This participation is not a separate or discrete but an integral part of their lives and continuing education. "Through their organizational lives people enhance their collectivist spirit and sense of discipline, strengthen solidarity and acquire consciousness of fulfilling their revolutionary duties," Kim Il-Sung reported.²¹ Recognizing that students don't constitute a class separate from workers in Korea, the study-work system includes "university-level factory colleges" where workers study after the workday."²² Kim Jong-Un affirmed the unity of organization and education in a text prepared for the 75th anniversary of the WPK's founding: "The solidity and strength of the party and all the success in a party depend on how the cadres and other members of the party are education and bound together organizationally and ideologically."²³

In a 1983 speech to the First Conference of Ministers of Education and Culture of Non-aligned and Other Developing

---

20   Helen-Louise Hunter, *Kim Il-Sung's North Korea* (Westport: Praeger, 1999), 56.

21   Kim Il-Sung, *On the Korean People's Struggle to Apply the Juche Idea* (Pyongyang: Foreign Languages Publishing House, 1983), 52.

22   Ibid., 54.

23   Kim Jung-Un, "The Workers' Party of Korea is the Party of the Great Leader Comrade Kim Il Sung," *Study of the Juche Idea* 91 (2020): 4.

Countries, Kim Il-Sung emphasized the priority of education above all else in the struggle for robust independence. Creating and reviving a revolutionary national culture is crucial, he insisted, in order to unify political and economic independence, and this in turn required education. "Our country's experience proves," he told the Ministers, "that in order to build an independent and sovereign country, national education must be kept ahead of all other work. Only when national education is developed on a priority basis to bring up people to be powerful beings equipped with independence and creativity and train a large number of native cadres, can we fully solve all problems arising in the building of a new society."[24] This task must not be delayed until the economic forces of society are built up. Even with few economic resources, education should be prioritized *now*.

As Kim Il-Sung notes in the following pages, it is the entirety of society which has to engage in the educational endeavor of defending the revolution, building communism, and maintaining independence. Those tasked with this project are, importantly, teachers—unlike in the U.S. where elite capitalists like Bill and Melinda Gates and a rung of bureaucratic administrators guide educational policy and practice.[25] It is teachers themselves who are literally responsible for educational work. The *Theses on Socialist Education* position teachers not as those who prepare students for standardized tests but rather as "career revolutionaries who bring up the younger generation to be successors to the revolution and communists." Yet it is not individual teachers but collectives of teachers who are all integrated into regular political

---

24   Kim Il-Sung, "For the Development of National Culture of Newly-Emerging Countries," in Kim-Il Sung, *Answers to the Questions Raised by Foreign Journalists* (Pyongyang: Foreign Languages Publishing House, 1991), 9.

25   Wayne Au, *Unequal by Design: High-Stakes Testing and the Standardization of Inequality* (New York: Routledge, 2009).

and social work who determine the appropriate pedagogy for the moment. The closing of the *Theses* again emphasizes that education is not the domain of younger people and teachers: "In a socialist society all members of society must take part in educational work," which is why the DPRK's educational system includes a continuing education department that organizes educational programs that are part of factories, agricultural collectives, fisheries, and other places of production.

To determine the appropriate pedagogy and curriculum, teachers themselves must engage in ongoing education, become more tightly involved in Party life and the people's organizations—all tasks that are part of a broader unity of socialist education. Teachers have to learn the WPK's orientations not by reading Party publications but by becoming more active in the Party. They have to continually raise their political and academic qualifications, the latter of which include their specialties as well as "various fields, including the elementary scientific knowledge," "the internal and external situation, the specific conditions in our country and educational theory and methods." This is done formally through teacher-training programs but also, importantly, by engaging in "the revolutionary habit of study," which means they "must study regularly, study energetically and read a great deal."[26]

THE ANTI-COMMUNISM OF CRITICAL PEDAGOGY

The relentless demonization of north Korea within the capitalist world stems from a number of interrelated factors. First, imperialist hostilities toward the DPRK stems from the centuries-old geopolitical significance of the Korean peninsula. Second, and this would be true even without the peninsula's geopolitical significance, the DPRK has been under attack for the

---

26   Kim Il-Sung, *Theses on Socialist Education* (Pyongyang: Foreign Languages Publishing House), 8-44.

simple fact that they are a socialist country. For global capitalism/imperialism, the existence of the socialist movement, at any level, from organizations within capitalist-dominated countries to socialist parties who hold state power, represents a real or potential threat to capital's internal drive to expand its reach and influence over every inch of the planet. The fact is that today the DPRK represents not only an actually-existing socialist country, but an actually-existing alternative to the neoliberal world order.

More specifically, however, the DPRK emerged after WWII during a global wave of socialist-inspired national liberation movements. Updating Lenin's theory of imperialism, Ghanian Pan-African revolutionary Kwame Nkrumah (1965/2004) referred to this era as neo-colonialism. Describing this era, Nkrumah noted that—following the emergence of the Soviet Union as well as the post-World War II rise of socialism in both Europe and China—capitalism had lost "'large sources of raw materials and financial investment and commodity markets [...] from its field of exploitation" with the emergence of the Soviet Union and then the rise of socialism in central and eastern Europe and China.[27]

Within this revolutionary and anti-colonial context, U.S. foreign policy sought, on one hand, to retain colonial domination by alternative means, and on the other, to tenaciously cling onto their remaining colonial holdings—including Korea. The U.S., desperate to take control of the entire peninsula, instigated the first global class war, the so-called Korean War. It was this war that birthed the military industrial complex, that unleashed for the first time new chemical weapons like Agent Orange, and that was fought precisely along class lines. That is, rather than the imperialist countries at war with each other over the colonial re-division of the world, for the first time capitalist countries lined up

---

27   Kwame Nkrumah, *Neo-Colonialism: The Last State of Imperialism* (London: PANAF, 1965/2004), 41.

on one side and socialist countries on the other in a global class war. To make sense of the on-going hysterical-level villainization of Korea, the country's modern history must be situated in this historical context.

Locating the demonization of DPRK within these efforts, Nkrumah explains how "this struggle has been given an ideological content by invoking anti-communism as the mainspring of the battle to bring the socialist sector of the globe back into the exploitative control Western financial monopoly." Anti-communism has commonly manifested itself in racist portrayals of north Korean leaders and government as unstable, irrational, and the Korean people as indoctrinated, mindless zombies. Attempting to turn reality on its head, the DPRK is painted as presenting a danger to the United States' national security as if the U.S. was somehow ever the victim.

Even so-called beacons of objective journalism such as *The New York Times* routinely publish racist articles arguing that millions of north Koreans are subjected to a totalizing, cradle-to-the-grave system of mind-control based on a cult of personality that demands complete, unwavering obedience. The imperialist narrative is based on the ridiculous assumption that the Korean people are required to accept the absolute glorification of the north Korean state, on one hand, and the fanatical hatred of the U.S., Japan, and south Korea on the other. During our visits to the primary, secondary, and higher education institutions of Chongryon, the General Association of Korean Residents in Japan, we saw textbooks that praised the civil rights movement in the U.S., portrayed the Koreans in the south as their siblings, and the history of progressive movements in Japan. The common depictions of mindless Koreans uncritically following the so-called most repressive regime in the world are nothing less than racist caricatures. Depicting the people of an entire country as naïve fools with no agency is certainly racist.

In the preface to his short, popularly-written book, *North Ko-*

rea, Bruce Cumings took note of the stark absence in the U.S. of any counter-arguments challenging the racist caricatures of the DPRK, even among progressives.[28] In fact, this anti-communism is precisely one of the motivations behind the founding theorists of "critical pedagogy" as an attempt to dismiss socialism and the legacy of revolutionary Marxism. It's important to clarify, however, that "critical pedagogy" was first coined in Henry Giroux's 1981 book, *Ideology, Culture, and the Process of Schooling.*[29] He furthered this line of critique in his 1983 book, *Theory and Resistance in Education,* which contends that post-World War II both the imperialist and capitalist states as well as the countries in the so-called socialist bloc, suffered from the exact same increasing alienation and the suppression of political and economic freedom through repression and authoritarian rule. There's no mention of the enormous gains made by socialist or newly-liberated countries around the globe.

This wasn't limited to Giroux. Stanley Aronowitz, an early theorist of critical pedagogy, formulated a political line against communism as it highlighted the "best aspects" of "American democracy." He wrote that "the Soviet Union is far from an egalitarian society; privilege and nepotism are rampant."[30] The case against socialist revolutions was part of his set-up to dismiss the history and theory of revolutionary Marxism.[31]

---

28 Bruce Cumings, *North Korea: Another Country* (New York: The New Press, 2004).

29 For more on this, see Curry S. Malott, *History and Education: Engaging the Global Class War* (New York: Peter Lang, 2015).

30 Stanley Aronowitz, *Crisis in Historical Materialism: Class, Politics and Culture in Marxist Theory* (St. Paul: University of Minnesota Press, 1979), 23.

31 Much of this was based on misreadings of secondary Marxist literature. See David I. Backer, "History of the Reproduction-Resistance Dichotomy in Critical Education: The Line of Critique Against Louis Althusser, 1974-1985," *Critical Education* 12, no. 6 (2021): 1-21.

Elsewhere, Curry has argued that critical pedagogy emerged as an intentional betrayal of the global class of working and oppressed people.[32] As people's movements in the U.S. and around the world suffered major counter-revolutionary setbacks, what remained of the left tended to break from Marxism-Leninism as it was pulled to the right.

There is a particularly striking irony here since critical pedagogy has always been a coin with at least two sides. Critical pedagogy was not only part of the larger move to the right, but it was also a challenge to the move to the right, popularly known as neoliberalism. The beginning of the neoliberal era in education is symbolized by Reagan's National Commission on Excellence in Education 1983 report *A Nation at Risk*. Mobilizing Cold War rhetoric, the White House and the Secretary of the Department of Education, Terrel Bell, in unprecedented fashion, blamed teachers and education for the economic recession of the 1970s.[33] The report claims the United States was falling behind its global competitors in education and technological innovation to such an extent that if it had been the result of an external imposition, it would have been considered an act of war.

Feeling directly threatened by this attack teachers and educators would join the critical pedagogy movement seeking understanding and action (*i.e.* theory and practice), only to find a critical pedagogy that functioned as the theoretical mechanism shifting the focus from class struggle and seizing state power to a form of liberalism focused on assimilating into, rather than dismantling and replacing, the global system of racist and sexist imperialism. In other words, it rejected outright the possibility or necessity for a revolutionary rupture, for the working and op-

---

32 See Curry S. Malott, "In Defense of Communism: Against Critical Pedagogy, Capitalism, and Trump," *Critical Education* 8, no. 1 (2017): 1-24.

33 Derek R. Ford, *Education and the Production of Space: Political Pedagogy, Geography, and Urban Revolution* (New York: Routledge, 2017), ch. 3.

pressed classes to overthrow their oppressors.

Again, however, as with the U.S. corporate media, popular culture, and the State Department, critical pedagogy has a sad history of either being cruel to north Korea or ignoring their existence and struggle completely. This is ironic and a missed opportunity because north Korea represents one of the "remaining self-proclaimed top-to-bottom alternative[s] to neoliberalism."[34]

Perhaps the worst position critical pedagogy takes lies in its lumping together of both left-wing and far-right countries; writing off both unequatable political regimes as simply "authoritarian." For example, north Korea has been put in the same category as Pakistan and India as countries with nuclear weapons who have threatened to use them. Joel Spring's *Wheels in the Head* denounces the DPRK even as the author seems to know little about the state and its ideology as, for instance, he mentions the "Korean Communist Party," which hasn't existed since August 1946.[35] In a disgustingly eurocentric and colonial gesture, Spring's critique of the socialist education system in the north is not only ahistoricized but is based primarily on Plato!

But the power and influence of U.S. imperialism continues to wane on the international stage. On the Korean peninsula, in particular, the south's successful Candlelight Movement in 2016 was responsible for the successful ousting of the repressive Park Geun-hye regime, which paved the way for the election of Moon Jae-in. Moon's administration has a much more progressive orientation and has made tremendous strides toward the peaceful reunification of the country, the normalization of relations with the north, and the campaign to get the U.S. to sign a peace treaty

---

34   Bruce Cumings, *North Korea: Another Country* (New York: The New Press, 2004), viii.

35   Joel Springs, *Wheels in the Head: Educational Philosophies of Authority, Freedom, and Culture from Confucianism to Human Rights*, 3rd ed. (New York: Routledge, 2008).

with the DPRK. In the north, the successful development of a nuclear armaments deterrent represents another major indicator that the global balance of power is shifting away from the imperialist centers of power.

Further evidence of this shift is the fact that the U.S. would come to the table in 2019 in a historic summit between U.S. President Donald Trump and DPRK leader Kim Jong-Un to discuss the peaceful reunification of a self-determined Korea. Although Trump's efforts were undermined by hard-right war hawks, the symbolic significance alone is undeniable.

It is precisely within this context of further global destabilization by U.S. imperialism, with Korea as a possible epicenter, that the works of Kim Il-Sung become increasingly relevant for countering the anti-communism aimed at Korean leaders. Such efforts challenge further U.S. aggressions while simultaneously revealing important lessons and insights from one of the great leaders, tacticians, and socialist thinkers of the twentieth century.

As a closing example, and despite grotesque caricatures of Korea and its leaders as doctrinaire, Kim Il-Sung's writings reveal deep, creative commitments—insights critical pedagogy would be wise to engage. Socialist pedagogy is not top-down but produced by the entirety of the society. Rather than the top leadership subjecting people to its dictates, the Party is the political collective of the entirety of society. It is this collective which educates itself, and which engages in endless "energetic study" in order to continue to inspire and to draw on the revolutionary enthusiasm of the people.

Dogmatism, according to Kim Il-Sung, is an enemy of the day-to-day assessment of the balance of forces needed in the creative, tactical process of leading a revolutionary, anti-colonial movement waged against powerful forces. In this context, dogmatically clinging to predetermined formulations can lead to catastrophe and the ultimate defeat of liberation forces. Because this dialectical truth holds true in any context and in any era, the works of the world's great dialecticians like Kim Il-Sung remain important sources for revolutionary socialist organizers, including those working in education.

We see that education is not a discrete area of revolutionary struggle, but one which is inseparable from the social, economic, and political developments of society. At the same time, education is a *fundamental* feature of such a unity, which is why, as Moe Taylor relays, Kim Il-sung would state even before the *Theses*, that north Korea's transition from a colonized and underdeveloped country into a strong national economy "was achieved 'by relying on the high revolutionary enthusiasm and limitless creativity of our people,' harness[ed] through mass mobilization campaigns."[36]

---

36 Moe Taylor. "Between Market Socialism and the New Man: Cuban and north Korean Economic Discourse in the 1960s," North Korean Review 17, no. 1 (2021): 13.

1

ON ELIMINATING DOGMATISM AND FORMALISM AND ESTABLISHING JUCHE IN OUR IDEOLOGICAL WORK

Kim Il-Sung

Editors' note: *This speech was delivered on December 28, 1955—just two years after the Korean People's Army kicked the U.S. out of their country and forced them to sign an armistice—to Party Propagandists and Agitators. It marks one of the most significant articulations of the concept of "Juche," which guides and informs almost all aspects of life and society in the DPRK. Juche was produced through decades of experience in complex and intricate struggles against the Korean Party's adversaries and within different trends in the Korean left. For more on the origins and context of Juche, see our introduction. We've added headings and minor edits into the text.*

INTRODUCTION

Today I want to address a few remarks to you on the shortcomings in our Party's ideological work and on how to eliminate them in the future.

As you learned at yesterday's session, there have been serious ideological errors on the literary front. It is obvious, then, that our propaganda work also cannot have been faultless. It is to be regretted that our propaganda work suffers in many respects from dogmatism and formalism.

The principal shortcomings in ideological work are the failure to delve deeply into all matters and the lack of *Juche*. It may not be proper to say *Juche* is lacking, but, in fact, it has not yet been firmly established. This is a serious matter. We must thoroughly rectify this shortcoming. Unless this problem is solved, we cannot hope for good results in ideological work.

Why does our ideological work suffer from dogmatism and formalism? And why do our propagandists and agitators fail to go deeply into matters, only embellishing the façade, and why do they merely copy and memorize foreign things, instead of working creatively? This offers us food for serious reflection.

What is *Juche* in our Party's ideological work? What are we doing? We are not engaged in any other country's revolution, but precisely in the Korean revolution. This, the Korean revolution, constitutes *Juche* in the ideological work of our Party. Therefore, all ideological work must be subordinated to the interests of the Korean revolution. When we study the history of the Communist Party of the Soviet Union, the history of the Chinese revolution, or the universal truth of Marxism-Leninism, it is all for the purpose of correctly carrying out our own revolution.

By saying that the ideological work of our Party lacks in *Juche*, I do not mean, of course, that we have not made the revolution or that our revolutionary work was undertaken by passers-by. Nonetheless, *Juche* has not been firmly established in ideological work, which leads to dogmatic and formalistic errors and does much harm to our revolutionary cause.

To make revolution in Korea we must know Korean history and geography and know the customs of the Korean people. Only then is it possible to educate our people in a way that suits them and to inspire in them an ardent love for their native place and their motherland.

It is of paramount importance to study, and widely publicize among the working people, the history of our country and of our people's struggle, before anything else.

Lessons from our Recent Revolutionary Experiences

This is not the first time we have raised this question. As far back as the autumn of 1945, that is, immediately after liberation, we emphasized the need to study the history of our nation's struggle and to inherit its fine traditions. Only when our people are educated in the history of their own struggle and its traditions, can their national pride be stimulated, and the broad masses be aroused to the revolutionary struggle.

Yet, many of our functionaries are ignorant of our country's history, and so do not strive to discover and carry forward its fine traditions. Unless this is corrected, it will lead, in the long run, to the negation of Korean history.

The mistakes made recently by Pak Chang Ok and his kind, too, may be attributed to their negation of the history of the Korean literary movement. They closed their eyes to the struggle of the fine writers of the KAPF—the Korean (Corean) Artiste Proletarienne Federation—and to the splendid works of Pak Yon Am, Chong Da San and other progressive scholars and writers of our country. We told them to make a profound study of those things and give them wide publicity, but they did not do so.

Today, ten years after liberation, we have all the conditions for collecting materials on our literary legacy and turning it to full use. Nevertheless, the propaganda workers remain wholly indifferent to this.

At the Fifth Plenary Meeting of the Party Central Committee, it was decided to actively publicize the history of our people's struggle and valuable cultural heritage, but workers in the field of propaganda failed to do so. They went so far as to forbid the newspapers to carry articles on the anti-Japanese struggle of the Korean people.

The Kwangju Student Incident, for example, was a mass struggle in which tens of thousands of Korean youths and students rose against Japanese imperialism; it played a big part in inspiring the anti-Japanese spirit in broad sections of the Korean youth. As a matter of course, we should publicize this movement widely and educate youth and students in the brave fighting spirit displayed by their forerunners. Our propaganda workers have failed to do so. Instead, Syngman Rhee has been making propaganda of this movement in his favour. This has created a false impression that the Communists disregard national traditions. What a dangerous thing! It will be impossible for us to win over the south Korean youth if we go on working in this way.

So far propaganda work in this respect has all been dropped and laid aside, though no one has ever given instructions to. Newspapers do not write about it, nor is any meeting held to commemorate it. Things like the Kwangju Student Incident ought to be taken up by the Democratic Youth League. The Kwangju Student Incident is an excellent example of the struggle of youth and students of our country against imperialism.

The same must be said of the June Tenth Independence Movement. This was another mass struggle in which the Korean people rose against Japanese imperialism. It is true that the struggle was greatly hampered by the factionalists who had slipped into it. Considering that even after liberation, the Pak Hon Yong-Li Sung Yop spy clique crept into our ranks and wrought mischief, it goes without saying that in those days the factionalists could carry on subversive activities more easily. But, even so, was the struggle itself wrong? No, it was not. Although the struggle ended in failure because of a few bad elements who had wormed their way into the leadership of the organization, we cannot deny its revolutionary character; we should learn a lesson from that failure.

No publicity has been given even to the March First Movement. If you work in this way, you cannot expect to lead along the right path with the progressive people who have a national consciousness, let alone the Communists. The lack of leadership by a Communist Party was the principal cause of the failure of the March First Movement. But who can ever deny the fact that the March First Movement was a nation-wide resistance movement against Japanese imperialism? We ought to explain to the people the historic significance of this movement and educate them by its lessons.

Many past revolutionary movements ended in failure in our country because of the scoundrels who managed to install themselves in the leadership of those movements, but there can be no denying the struggles waged by the people on those occasions. The popular masses always fought well with courage. Pak Chang Ok may have denied this arbitrarily. But no true Marxist-Leninist dare deny the people's exploits in their struggles.

When I asked Pak Chang Ok and his followers why they rejected the "KAPF," they answered that they did so because some renegades were involved in it. Then, did they mean to say that the "KAPF," in which Comrade Li Gi Yong and other prominent proletarian writers of our country worked as its very core, was an organization of no importance? We must highly value the fighting achievements of those people, and develop our literature around them.

What assets do we have for carrying on the revolution if the history of our people's struggle is denied? If we cast aside all these things, it would mean that our people did nothing. There are many things to be proud of in our country's peasant movements of the past. In recent years, however, no articles dealing with them have appeared in our newspapers.

In schools, too, there is a tendency to neglect lectures on Korean history. During the war the curricula of the Central Party School allotted 160 hours a year to the study of world history, but very few hours were given to Korean history. This is how things were done in the Party school, and so it is quite natural that our functionaries are ignorant of their own country's history.

In our propaganda and agitation work, there are numerous examples of extolling only foreign things, while slighting our own.

Once I visited a People's Army vacation home, where a picture of the Siberian steppe was hung. That landscape probably pleases the Russians. But the Korean people prefer the beautiful scenery of our own country. There are beautiful mountains such as Mts. Kumgang-san and Myohyang-san in our country; there are clear streams, the blue sea with its rolling waves and the fields with ripening crops. If we are to inspire in our People's Armymen a love for their native place and their country, we must show them many pictures of such landscapes of our country.

One day this summer when I dropped in at a local democratic publicity hall, I saw diagrams of the Soviet Union's Five-Year Plan shown there, but not a single diagram illustrating the Three-Year Plan of our country. Moreover, there were pictures of huge factories in foreign countries, but there was not a single one of the factories we were rehabilitating or building. They do not even put up any diagrams and pictures of our economic construction, let alone study the history of our country.

I noticed in a primary school that all the portraits hanging on the walls were of foreigners such as Mayakovsky, Pushkin, etc., and there were none of Koreans. If children are educated in this way, how can they be expected to have national pride?

Here is a ridiculous example. Even in attaching a table of contents to a booklet, foreign ways are aped and it is put in the back. We should learn, as a matter of course, from the good experience of socialist construction, but what on earth is the need of putting the table of contents in the back of a booklet in foreign style? This does not suit the taste of Koreans. As a matter of course, we should put it in the front of a book, shouldn't we?

In compelling schoolbooks, too, materials are not taken from our literary works but from foreign ones. All this is due to the lack of *Juche*.

JUCHE AND OUR PARTY WORK

The lack of *Juche* in propaganda work has done much harm to Party work. For the same reason, many comrades do not respect our revolutionaries. At present more than 100 comrades who took part in revolutionary struggles in the past are attending the Central Party School; until recently they had been buried in obscurity.

We sent many revolutionaries to the Ministry of the Interior, but many of them were dismissed on the ground that they were incompetent. At the Central Party School, I once met a comrade who had formerly taken part in revolutionary activities; he had been left in his post as chief of a county interior service station for eight years. This is quite an improper attitude toward revolutionaries.

Today our functionaries have become so insolent that they show no respect for their seniors. They have been allowed to fall into such a habit, whereas Communists naturally have a higher moral sense than any other people and hold their revolutionary seniors in high esteem.

In our People's Army, a vigorous struggle has been waged to uphold the revolutionary traditions and, as a result, most of the people who had taken part in revolutionary activities have become either regimental or divisional commanders.

If we had not organized the People's Army with old revolutionary cadres as its core, what would have been the outcome of the last war? It would have been impossible for us to defeat the enemy and win a great victory under such difficult conditions.

During our retreat certain foreigners predicted that most of our army units, trapped by enemy encirclement, would not be able to get back. But we were firmly convinced that all of them would manage to come back. In fact, they all did return, with the exception of the dead. The foreigners were greatly impressed at this and said there were few armies like ours in the world. How did this come about? The explanation is that our army cadres were comrades who in the past had taken part in guerrilla warfare or in local revolutionary movements. That is precisely why our army is strong.

Ten years have passed now since our Party was founded. Therefore, the Party members should naturally be educated in the history of our Party. If our functionaries are not educated in the revolutionary history of our country, they will be unable to carry forward our fine revolutionary traditions, nor will they be able to realize which direction to take in their revolutionary activities.

Establishing *Juche* as a Political and Ideological Framework

We should study our own things in earnest and be versed in them. Otherwise, we shall be unable to solve creatively in keeping with our actual conditions the new problems that confront us one after another in practice.

As a matter of fact, the form of our government should also be fitted to the specific conditions of our country. Does our people's power have exactly the same form as in other socialist countries? No, it does not. They are alike in that they are based on Marxist-Leninist principles, but their forms are different. No doubt, our platform, too, is in keeping with the realities of our country. Our 20-Point Platform is the development of the Programme of the Association for the Restoration of the Fatherland. As you all know, the Association for the Restoration of the Fatherland existed before our country was liberated.

Our functionaries often commit errors due to lack of a clear understanding of these matters.

Some people even think it strange that the agricultural

co-operative movement is progressing rapidly in our country. There is nothing strange about this. In the very past, the economic foundation of the Korean peasantry was very weak, and the land was barren. Under Japanese imperialism, the peasant movement developed, and the revolutionary spirit of the peasantry ran very high. What is more, the peasants were tempered politically through the democratic construction after liberation and during the bitter war. So, it is natural that the agricultural co-operative movement should be making rapid progress in our country today.

Comrade Pak Yong Bin, on returning from the Soviet Union, said that since the Soviet Union was following the line of easing international tension, we should also drop our slogan against U.S. imperialism. Such an assertion has nothing to do with revolutionary vigilance. The U.S. imperialists scorched our land, slaughtered our innocent people *en masse*, and are still occupying the southern half of our country. They are our sworn enemy, aren't they?

It is utterly ridiculous to think that our people's struggle against the U.S. imperialists conflicts with the efforts of the Soviet people to ease international conflicts with the efforts of the Soviet people to ease international tension. Our people's condemnation and struggle against the aggressive policy of the U.S. imperialists towards Korea are not contradictory, but conducive to the struggle of the people of the world for lessening international tension and for defending peace. At the same time, the struggle of the peace-loving people the world over, including the Soviet people, to ease tension creates more favourable conditions for the anti-imperialists struggle of our people.

Pak Chang Ok was ideologically linked to the reactionary bourgeois writer Li Tae Jun in that he did not try to study the history of our country and our realities. Besides the remnants of bourgeois ideology in his mind, he had the conceited idea that he knew everything without even studying the realities of our country. Consequently, things went wrong. The harm he did to our ideological work is very serious.

After liberation he and his ilk said that Li Gwang Su was a talented man, and that, therefore, it would be advisable to give him prominence. But I pointed out it would be wrong to do so. Li Gwang Su wrote a novel, *The Wife of a Revolutionary*, in which he insulted the revolutionaries discharged from prison. Li Gwang Su was a villain who used to rave that the Korean people and the Japanese imperialists came from "one and the same ancestry and roots." Therefore, I told them that it was totally unthinkable to give prominence to such a man, and never allowed them to do so.

Some comrades working in the Propaganda Department of the Party tried to copy mechanically from the Soviet Union in all their work. This was also because they had no intention to study our realities and lacked the true Marxist-Leninist spirit of educating the people in our own merits and in the traditions of our revolution. Many comrades swallow Marxism-Leninism whole, instead of digesting and assimilating it. It is therefore self-evident that they are unable to display revolutionary initiative.

We have so far failed to take measures for a systematic study of our country's history and our national culture. It has been ten years since liberation. And yet, we have failed to tackle the matter energetically; we have conducted it only in a hit-or-miss way. We had few cadres before, but now we have scholars, funds and materials, and have sufficient conditions FOR conducting it. This is quite possible if only you make a good study and organize the work. Every effort should be made to unearth our national legacies and carry them forward. True, we should be active in learning from what is progressive internationally. But we should develop fine things of our own while introducing advanced culture. Otherwise, our people will lose faith in their own ability and become a spineless people who only try to copy others.

Hearing us say that it is necessary to establish *Juche*, some comrades might take it simply and form a wrong idea that we need not learn from foreign countries. That would be quite wrong. We must learn from the good experiences of socialist countries.

The important thing is to know what we are learning from. The aim we pursue in learning is to turn the advanced experience of the Soviet Union and other socialist countries to a good account in our Korean revolution.

During the war, Ho Ga I, Kim Jae Uk and Pak Il U once quarrelled stupidly among themselves over the problems of how to carry on political work in the army. Those from the Soviet Union insisted upon the Soviet method and those from China stuck to the Chinese method. So they quarrelled, some advocating the Soviet fashion and others the Chinese way. That was sheer nonsense.

It does not matter whether you use the right hand or the left, whether you use a spoon or chopsticks at the table. No matter how you eat, it is all the same insofar as food is put into your mouth, isn't it? What is the need of being particular about "fashion" in wartime? When we carry on political work to strengthen our People's Army and win battles, any method will do so long as our aim is achieved. Yet Ho Ga I and Pak Il U squabbled about such a trifle. This only weakens discipline within the Party. At that time the Party centre maintained that we should learn all the good things from both the Soviet Union and China and, on this basis, work out a method of political work suitable to the actual conditions of our country.

It is important in our work to grasp revolutionary truth, Marxist-Leninist truth, and apply it correctly to the actual conditions of our country. There can be no set principle that we must follow the Soviet pattern. Some advocate the Soviet way and others the Chinese, but it is not high time to work out our own?

Towards an Internationalist and Independent Revolution

The point is that we should not mechanically copy forms and methods of the Soviet Union, but should learn from its experience in struggle and Marxist-Leninist truth. So, while learning from the experience of the Soviet Union, we must put stress not on the forms but on learning the essence of its experience.

In learning from the experience of the Soviet Union there is a marked tendency just to model after the external forms. Once *Pravda* puts out a headline "A Day in Our Country," our *Rodong Sinmun* carries the same title: "A Day in Our Country." What is the use of copying even this sort of thing? The same is true of clothing. When there are very graceful Korean costumes for our women, what is the use of discarding them and putting on dresses which are unbecoming of them? There is no need to do this. I suggested to Comrade Pak Jon Ae to see that our women dress in Korean costumes as far as possible.

Just copying the forms used by others instead of learning Marxist-Leninist truth brings us no good, only harm.

Both in revolutionary struggle and in construction work, we should firmly adhere to Marxist-Leninist principles, applying them in a creative manner to suit the specific conditions of our country and our national characteristics.

If we mechanically apply foreign experience, disregarding the history of our country and the traditions of our people and without taking account of our own realities and level of preparedness of our people, dogmatic errors will result, and much harm will be done to the revolutionary cause. To do so is not fidelity to Marxism-Leninism nor to internationalism; it runs counter to them.

Marxism-Leninism is not a dogma; it is a guide to action and a creative theory. So, Marxism-Leninism can display its indestructible vitality only when it is applied creatively to suit the specific conditions of each country. The same applies to the experience of the fraternal parties. It will prove valuable to us only when we make a study of it, grasp its essence, and properly apply it to our realities. Instead, if we just gulp it down and spoil our work, it will not only harm our work but also lead to discrediting the valuable experience of the fraternal parties.

In connection with the problem of establishing *Juche* I think it necessary to touch on internationalism and patriotism.

Internationalism and patriotism are inseparably linked with each other. You must know that the love of Korean Communists for their country does not go against the internationalism of the working class but conforms fully with it. To love Korea is just as good as to love the Soviet Union and the socialist camp and, likewise, to love the Soviet Union and the socialist camp means precisely loving Korea. They constitute a complete whole. For the great cause of the working class has no frontiers and our revolutionary cause is a part of the international revolutionary cause of the working class throughout the world. The one supreme goal of the working class of all countries is to build a communist society. The difference, if any, lies only in the fact that certain countries do this earlier and others later.

It would be wrong to advocate patriotism alone and neglect internationalist solidarity. For the victory of the Korean revolution and for the great cause of the international working class, we should strengthen solidarity with the Soviet people, our liberator and helper, and with the peoples of all the socialist countries. This is our sacred internationalist duty. The Soviet people, on their part, are doing all they can to consolidate solidarity not only with the countries of the socialist camp but also with the working class of the whole world both for communist construction in their country and for the victory of world revolution.

Thus, patriotism and internationalism are inseparable. He who does not love his own country cannot be loyal to internationalism, and he who is unfaithful to internationalism cannot be faithful to his own country and people. A true patriot is precisely an internationalist and vice versa.

If we cast aside all that is good in our country and only copy and memorize foreign things in ideological work, it will certainly bring losses to our revolution, and thereby prevent us from properly carrying out our internationalist obligations to the international revolutionary cause.

In the report to the Second Party Congress, I quoted the following passage from the statement of the Commander of the Soviet army published on the first day of its entry into our country: "Korean people!...You have happiness in your own hands.... Koreans must make themselves the creators of their own happiness." This statement is perfectly correct, and if we fail to act accordingly, we may lose broad segments of the masses.

The formalism of our propaganda workers also finds expression in exaggerating things in propaganda work. For example, such bombastic expressions as "all have risen," "all have been mobilized," etc., have long been in fashion in speeches and articles.

We advised Pak Chong Ok more than once against it. Pak Chang Ok made mistakes because he could not break away from "all" type of bombast he had created. Later, he took a fancy to the superlative of the Chinese ideograph "great," and abused the adjective "great." I do not know whether this practice was due to his ignorance of Chinese ideographs or to his erroneous ideological viewpoint.

When propaganda work is conducted with such exaggeration without any substance to it, it will lead people to be carried away by victory and to become easy-going. This bad practice is also responsible for the false reports handed in by junior officials.

The use of an adjective may seem a simple matter, but when wrongly used it may cause our work to fail. In future, such a practice should be discontinued thoroughly.

Now, I would like to refer to a few other immediate problems in ideological work.

The Party Central Committee has issued written material on the character and tasks of our revolution to help study the documents of its April Plenary Meeting. So, I will not make any further comment on this.

I would like to stress once more the prospects of the revolution in our country. Our revolution has two prospects. One is the peaceful reunification of our country, and the other its reunification under the conditions in which the forces of imperialism are sharply weakened by a big war.

We, of course, have been striving with all our might to bring about the first prospect.

Our struggle for the peaceful reunification of our country boils down to two points — to carry on construction successfully in the northern half and to conduct effective political work towards the southern half. If we fortify the democratic base by promoting socialist construction in the northern half and arouse the people in the southern half to the liberation struggle through effective political work directed to the southern half, the peaceful reunification of our country can be realized.

JUCHE AND THE STRUGGLE FOR PEACEFUL REUNIFICATION

Political work towards the southern half means strengthening the influence of the northern half and inducing its broad popular masses to support us. To this end, socialist construction in the northern half should be carried on successfully. The living standard of the people should be raised, and the economic foundation strengthened in the northern half through successful economic construction, and the entire people should be rallied around our Party. Then, no matter how desperately Syngman Rhee may try, he will never be able to dampen the fighting spirit of the people in the southern half who are constantly inspired by the socialist construction in the northern half.

A man who came over from the southern half some time ago said: "Syngman Rhee says in his propaganda that the northern half has a population of only 3 million and there is nothing left in Pyongyang but heaps of ashes. But I have seen here that the bridge over the River Taedong-gang has been restored to its former state and Pyongyang is being built into a much more beautiful city than ever before. Syngman Rhee has told a whopping lie." This is what will happen when we carry on construction successfully.

In 1948 when a joint conference of political parties and social organizations from north and south Korea was held, we did not have much to our credit in construction in the northern half. But all the Right-wing personalities of south Korea came to us with the exception of Syngman Rhee and Kim Song Su. The joint conference was of very great significance. Many of those who came to the northern half at that time remained here.

This is what Kim Gu said: "I have found north Korea to my liking. I have seen many Communists both in Shanghai and in south Korea (if he met any, they must have been those of the Tuesday group or the M-L group), but north Korean Communists are different. I thought before that Communists were narrow-minded and wicked people, but as I have found here this time, you are broad-minded and generous people with whom I can fully cooperate. I will cooperate with you by all means. I am old now and have no ambition for power. If I do not go back to south Korea, Syngman Rhee will certainly clamour that I have been detained. And it is my desire to go back and give publicity to the fine things I have seen here. So I must go back at any rate. Do not think that I am going to collaborate with the Yankees. When I return here later, please give me an apple orchard, as I want to live in peace in the countryside for the rest of my life." Kim Gyu Sik, too, spoke in the same vein. After that, Kim Gu fought against the Yankees.

As you all know, Kim Gu was a nationalist. From the beginning he was against both imperialism and communism and came to us with the intention of negotiating with Communists. In view of the fact that even Kim Gu who had regarded communism as an inveterate enemy changed his view of our endeavors to build up the country, it is quite easy to imagine what the workers, peasants, and the public figures with a national conscience in south Korea will think once they come and see the northern half.

Before liberation, the mere words that in the Soviet Union the working class held power and was building socialism made us yearn boundlessly for the Soviet Union where we had never been. How then can the people in the southern half possibly help yearning for the socialist construction of our people in the northern half who are of the same ethnical stock with them?

That is why successful construction in the northern half is more important than anything else.

As can be seen from the above, when the people in the southern half are roused to action against U.S. imperialism and the Syngman Rhee regime by successful socialist construction in the northern half and through effective political work directed towards the southern half, the peaceful reunification of our country can be materialized. This is the internal factor making it possible to achieve peaceful reunification.

The external factor conducive to the country's peaceful reunification should likewise be taken into consideration. If we succeed in maintaining peace for a five to ten years period, China, with her more than 600 million population, will grow incomparably in might, not to mention the Soviet Union, and the power of the whole socialist camp will be further strengthened.

Parallel with the growth of the might of the socialist camp, the national-liberation movement of the peoples in the colonial and dependent countries has been ever more intensified, and many countries have achieved national independence. The peoples of India, Indonesia, Burma and other independent states in Asia and the peoples of the Arab countries are fighting for peace against imperialist aggression.

All this is a telling blow to imperialism, especially U.S. imperialism. When the forces of peace, democracy and socialism grow stronger, the U.S. imperialists will finally be compelled to withdraw from Korea.

Of course, the struggle for the country's peaceful reunification is an arduous and protracted one. But when we grow stronger and the forces of peace, democracy and socialism are further strengthened internationally, we will be able to achieve peaceful reunification. This is one prospect of the development of the revolution in Korea and of the country's reunification.

The problem of the country's reunification might also be solved not by peaceful means but by war. If the imperialists were to unleash a war on a world-wide scale, we would have no alternative but to fight, and then it would be quite possible for us to fight and defeat the U.S. imperialists in Korea by our own strength. Although it would be somewhat hard for us to fight against U.S. imperialism single-handed, we should be able to defeat it rather easily when it is compelled to disperse its forces all over the world. In that case, we shall sweep the forces of U.S. imperialism from Korea and achieve the reunification of the country. This is the other prospect of the development of the Korean revolution and the reunification of the country.

We, however, do not want this prospect. We desire the first prospect, that is, reunification by peaceful means, and we are struggling for its realization.

No matter what the prospects of the country's reunification may be, it is more important than anything else to strengthen our Party and steal the Party spirit of its members.

In case negotiations start between the north and south, and then the barriers between them are torn down and we come to work among south Koreans, will it not be necessary for our Party to be strong? Only when our Party is strong, can it take advantage of such a favourable situation.

The proportion of our Party membership to the population is now one to ten, the membership being one million out of a population of 10 million. Indeed, this is not a small proportion. But, when compared with the total population of Korea, 30 million, one million is by no means large.

In south Korea the growth of the Party's force cannot help but be seriously limited, because the underground movement is conducted there in extremely difficult circumstances.

After reunification, it will be difficult to carry on our work with a small number of Party members, although the number will grow in south Korea, too. What is wrong with our training a large number of Party members in the far northern half from now on and assigning them evenly to work in the north and south after reunification? There is nothing wrong in this. Yet, at the time of the Fourth Plenary Meeting of the Party Central Committee Ho Ga I insisted that the Party close its doors in spite of the fact that it had a membership of no more than 600,000. Then the Party criticized his view and has since continued to increase its membership.

EDUCATION AND *JUCHE*

The point now is to give a good education to our one million Party members. Among our members there can sometimes be found those who even lag behind the non-Party masses. But even so, these people must not be expelled from the Party. They must be kept in the Party and educated; if they were expelled, our Party's strength might be weakened. This is all the more so since ours is not the only party.

It is our invariable organizational line to train the nuclei of the cells constantly while building up a mass party. By the nuclei we mean those Party members who are aware of communist truth and are capable of holding to the road of revolution without vacillating. It is difficult to arm the one million Party members overnight with an equal degree of communist consciousness. We must follow the line of training the nuclei first and then gradually raising the level of consciousness of all Party members.

Our line is to educate Party members with the help of core members. So, since the Fourth Plenary Meeting the Party has put special emphasis on the question of training the core members of the cells. It will be all the more gratifying if their number increases from five today to ten tomorrow and thus all Party members become core element, and even if not all but only 50 per cent of the Party membership does so, it will be a good thing.

In the development of our Party into a mass political party, the merging of the Communist Party and the New Democratic Party was of great significance. As a result of our correct organizational line and energetic struggle to win over the broad working masses, our Party has now developed into a mass political party embracing one million members. This success has by no means been easy to gain but has been achieved through extremely hard struggles.

We demand and fight for democratic rights and liberties in south Korea—freedom of speech, the press, assembly, and association—which are perquisites for the peaceful reunification of the country. We aim at securing conditions for our own free activities in the southern half while allowing political parties of south Korea to conduct political activities freely in the northern half.

When a situation is thus created for free political struggle in the north and the south, whoever wins over more of the masses will win the day. Therefore, it is of the greatest importance to strengthen our Party and the Party spirit of its members.

In order to steel the Party spirit of our members, we should have all of them make a constant and deep study of the documents of the Fourth and Fifth Plenary Meetings of the Party Central Committee.

Our comrades must direct more efforts to the organizational

and propaganda work of the Party, instead of being engrossed only in economic campaigns. Party cells must be built up well and Party members educated through the nuclei of the cells. It is particularly necessary to temper the Party spirit of those members who hold leading posts—ministers, vice-ministers, and bureau directors. Vigorous educational measures should be taken to fortify the Party spirit of the entire membership.

Our Party's composition is very complex. All sorts of people have joined our Party—those who once belonged to the Tuesday group and the M-L group, those who were affiliated with the Toiling People's Party after liberation, and others. Many were under the influence of the fractional elements in the past. These people are to be found both among responsible cadres in the central organs and among the members of the Party Central Committee.

Not all of the people are worthless. Education will make them all useful. But this education must not be conducted through a short-term campaign. Long, persistent education and criticism are needed.

A determined struggle must be fought to arm every Party member firmly with our Party's ideology and eliminate all remnants of bourgeois ideology persisting in the minds of Party members and working people. The Party spirit of our members should be tempered thoroughly, until their shortcomings and ideological maladies are completely remedied.

We were too late in criticizing Pak Chang Ok and Ki Sok Bok. If they had been criticized at the time of the Fifth Plenary Meeting of the Party Central Committee, things would not have gone so far. Therefore, it is especially important to remould the ideas of those leading cadres who have been influenced by Ho Ga I or Pak Il U and help them establish the Party's ideological system. This work must be undertaken by the Department of Organizational Leadership and the Propaganda and Agitation Department of the Party.

What is important in the education of Party members is to make them, especially the cadres, establish a mass viewpoint. Because this is lacking, bureaucracy continues to manifest itself. This is a grave shortcoming in our Party work.

In order to achieve our lofty aims of reunifying the country and building socialism and communism, we must win over the masses. We must clearly know what great losses bureaucracy can cause to the revolution.

Listening to the voices of the masses and championing their interests is an entirely different matter from basing one's work on misleading opinions currently in the streets. The latter has nothing in common with the revolutionary mass viewpoint. By the masses we mean the main masses we are relying on—the workers and peasants, and our allies who support and follow us. We should listen to them and defend their interests. Everyone, whether a Party worker, an administrative official or a functionary in a social organization, must work consistently in the interests of the revolution and the masses.

How was it possible for the anti-Japanese guerrillas to hold out for a long time? Why was it that the Japs failed to destroy us although they had a formidable armed force? Because the guerrillas had the correct mass viewpoint and the support of the masses. When we were wounded and entered a village, the peasants took care of us as though we were their own sons; they would manage to get rice, which they could hardly afford themselves, and boil it for us. Even the peasants living inside the earthen walls of the concentrated villages set up by the Japs, managed to send food to us outside the walls.

The masses supported and protected us in this way, because we had always defended their interests and fought for them at the risk of our own lives. All Party members have to learn from the attitude of the guerrillas towards the masses.

In the days of Japanese imperialist rule everything was imposed upon us by force—compulsory military service, compulsory labour draft, compulsory delivery of farm produce, etc. We are resolutely opposed to such practices.

A party divorced from the masses is like a fish out of water. With whom can the party carry out the revolution if not with the masses? Such a party will not only be unable to win in the revolution, but also will eventually find its very existence endangered.

It is solely for the purpose of protecting the interests of the masses that the party puts forward its programme and seizes state power. Therefore, would it not be against the aims of the party and the revolution to encroach on the interests of the masses?

Our laws and decisions are indisputably excellent. But all this will come to nothing if, in the course of putting them into effect, our functionaries impinge on the interests of the masses. You must bear this in mind and further strengthen educational work among Party members so that they can liquidate bureaucracy and acquire a correct mass viewpoint. If at least 50 per cent of all Party members acquire a correct mass viewpoint, it will mean a great change for our Party.

At present quite a few Party members are not firmly equipped with a correct mass viewpoint. The situation is especially worse among the cadres. Whether a Party member has a correct mass viewpoint or not also depends on his Party spirit. So tempering Party spirit is also of decisive importance in this respect.

Further, it is important to cultivate faith and optimism regarding the prospects of the revolution in the minds of the Party members. Without firm faith in the final victory of our cause and without optimism regarding the future of the revolution, under any and all circumstances, it would be impossible to overcome the difficulties one inevitably encounters in the course of the revolutionary struggle.

In order to make our Party members indomitable fighters who are always optimistic about the future of the revolution, it is necessary to intensify their Marxist-Leninist education. Without a clear understanding of the laws of social development and the inevitability of the triumph of socialism and communism, one can neither have faith in victory nor have the high-toned spirit and combativeness to withstand any difficulty.

Let me take an example of vacillation and defection in the ranks of the revolutionaries that was caused by a lack of knowledge of the laws of social development and of clear understanding of the trend of developments in a complex situation.

When the defeat of Japanese imperialism was near in sight, some people in the guerrilla detachments lost faith and deserted. This was partly because of certain formalistic defects in our propaganda work at that time. In those days propaganda about the Soviet Union was of special importance, and this is how we propagandized:

> A big clash will certainly occur some day between the Soviet Union and the imperialist states, because fundamental contradictions exist between them. Then, Japanese imperialism will perish and our country will be able to achieve independence.

That was wrong. Though we were right in our propaganda about the contradictions between the socialist state and the imperialist countries, we failed to propagandize the truth about the developments. As a result, when in 1941 a treaty of neutrality was concluded between the Soviet Union and Japan and a non-aggression pact between the Soviet Union and Hitler Germany was signed, some elements in the ranks of the guerrillas lost hope for the future and faltered. These waverers deserted our ranks, saying that after 10 years with the guerrillas, they had a dark future, uncertain whether they would have to spend another 10 or 20 years there. So we explained the revolutionary situation and the truth of revolution fully to the guerrillas. After that, there were no more deserters.

There is no doubt that sooner or later we shall see a great revolutionary event. That event, as I have already said, may either occur peacefully or non-peacefully. Whatever form the event may take, we must always be prepared to meet it.

In order to meet this great revolutionary event, the Party spirit of the Party members should be steeled; they should be educated to have a correct mass viewpoint and to have faith in victory and optimism regarding the future of the revolution.

Another important thing is to struggle properly against all sorts of anti-Party tendencies. If we had not had the experience of fighting the *Minsaengdan* in Kando before, we would not have been able to give appropriate leadership to the struggle against the counter-revolutionaries in Korea, especially during the war.

The Japanese organized a counter-revolutionary espionage organization called *Mingsaengdan* and smuggled it into the revolutionary districts in Kando. Then they resorted to the vile trick of alienating the Koreans from the Chinese and inciting strife among the Koreans. For some time those in the revolutionary camp fell victim to the enemy's crafty scheme, going the length of killing one another. As a result, many people lost their lives without any justification.

This experience proved very useful when we dealt with the case of the Pak Hon Yong clique. We adhered strictly to the principle of drawing a sharp distinction between spies and non-spies. We emphasized this many times in the Political Committee. There was a danger that we might possibly play into the hands of the Yankees and ruin many persons.

Of course, there must be a relentless struggle. Otherwise, some spies may escape punishment. But the struggle must always be carried on as an ideological struggle.

Those who were influenced by Pak Hon Yong cannot all be his ilk or spies. But his ideological influence still remains in the minds of these people. We must fight against this.

The experience acquired in the course of the struggle against the Park Hon Yong clique and in the counter-espionage campaigns should be made fully known to the Party members so that they may wage a rigorous struggle against espionage agents and correctly distinguish the spies from others. If you do not do so and suspect everybody, in the end you will find yourselves suspicious of your own shadow.

The enemy always plots to make people distrust one another and set them at odds with each other to disintegrate our ranks from within. You must learn to discern clearly and to combat such plots and slanders by the counter-revolutionaries. Party members should be educated in such a way that they can distinguish spies, waverers, nepotists, parochialists and factionalists.

Toward the Future

Such a struggle can be conducted properly only when the cadres and all the members of the Party are on a high level. Without attaining a high level of Marxist-Leninist knowledge, Party members cannot properly carry out such a difficult duty. In order to enable them to fight skillfully against the counter-revolutionaries, it is necessary to intensify their Marxist-Leninist education and, at the same time, to acquaint them extensively with the experience of the fight against the counter-revolutionaries.

Further, the work of propaganda and agitation should be stepped up among the broad masses. Education of the masses of the people in socialist ideology should be the main content of the work of propaganda and agitation. What is most important in this connection is to give the workers and peasants, especially the workers, a clear understanding that they are masters of power. When they have such intense consciousness, the workers will do everything as masters—take good care of their places of work, machines, and equipment, work hard, maintain good discipline, and effectively combat counter-revolutionaries.

The same is true of the peasants. If they realize that the working class is not only their ally but also their leader, and that they too are masters of power, the peasants will work their land well, take good care of their implements and willingly pay the tax in kind.

Everyone will show enthusiasm when he realizes that he is a master. When we were engaged in revolutionary activities in the past, who could ever have got us to do so for money? We fought without sleep, forgetting hunger, because we had realized that by making a revolution, we could not only improve our own lot but also save our country. The workers will likewise throw all their energy and zeal into their work when they become clearly aware that their labour is for their own happiness and for the prosperity of society.

Long, persistent education is needed to get all the working people to have such consciousness. We must patiently educate the masses and unite them around our Party still more closely.

In conclusion, I would like to make a few remarks about our newspapers. Our papers still fail to discharge their duties fully.

The central task of *Rodong Sinmun*, our Party organ, is to educate the Party members through day-to-day explanation of the Party's lines and policies and their fighting tasks; the central task of *Minju Choson* is to mobilize the masses to implement the policies of the state by explaining to them and giving them a full understanding of the laws and regulations of the people's power and the policies of the state. The organs of the General Federation of Trade Unions, the Democratic Youth League, and other organizations should likewise be edited in accordance with their respective characteristics and tasks.

Our newspapers have no specific features to distinguish one from another. This is a big failing. Whether this is because they are all furnished with material by the Korean Central News Agency or because some of them are limited in space, I do not know.

Here too, much formalism and dogmatism are noted. I think it necessary for you to look into this matter seriously.

I have so far touched upon some problems arising in the

ideological work of our Party. I hope you will take account of them, eliminate the shortcomings hitherto revealed and strive to raise our Party's ideological work to a higher level.

2

ON PUBLISHING *THE THESES ON SOCIALIST EDUCATION*

Kim Il-Sung

Editors' note: *This speech, delivered at the 14th Plenary Meeting of the Fifth Central Committee of the Workers' Party of Korea on September 05, 1977, introduces the* Theses on Socialist Education *and provides crucial background context for the proposal.*

In connection with the presentation of the *Theses on Socialist Education* at this plenary meeting of the Party Central Committee, I would like to speak briefly about its aims.

After the working class overthrows the capitalist system and establishes the socialist system, it is, of course, important to improve the material standard of living of the people through constructing a sound socialist economy. But it is no less important to increase the people's ideological consciousness and raise their cultural and technical levels.

We should steadily increase the ideological consciousness of the working people and raise their cultural and technical levels in order to make effective use of, and manage well, the existing material and technical foundations of our country and further consolidate and develop them.

As everyone knows, all the material wealth of a society comes as a result of the creative labour of the working masses. Only when the working masses become politically conscious of their status as the masters of society and reach high cultural and technical levels can they give full scope to their creative talents and enthusiasm in the building of socialism. Without increasing their ideological consciousness and raising their cultural and technical levels, the working people cannot play their role as the masters of society to the full. Then, socialist construction may simply stand still or even go into reverse. Therefore, after the working class has assumed power and established the socialist system, education conforming to socialist society should be given.

Even after its seizure of power, the working class has to build socialism for a long time against a capitalist background. Under such circumstances, bourgeois reactionary ideas and degenerate culture can infiltrate from outside, and internally all sorts of obsolete notions, including feudal and capitalist ones, may raise their heads. Therefore, the working-class party and state should pay particular attention to strengthening socialist education. If they do not conduct education commensurate with socialist society, but offer a motley education which is neither socialist nor capitalist, they will be unable to prevent the ideological and cultural infiltration of capitalism and the corrosive action of the surviving old ideas.

During the transition period from capitalism to socialism and communism, proper socialist education is essential for making every member of society revolutionary, working-class and communist.

Whether the working class has seized power in a developed capitalist country or a backward colonial, semi-feudal country, strengthening socialist education is always very important. The length of the transition period may differ from one country to another and be either long or short, depending on the level of development of the productive forces, but the educational work for remoulding the thinking of the people is a prominent matter in every country.

The revolutionary enthusiasm of the people runs very high when they struggle to overthrow the exploiting system and free themselves from exploitation and oppression, but it gradually declines after they have overthrown the system of exploitation and laid the material and technical foundations of the new society to a certain extent. Both the experience of those countries which carried out the socialist revolution a long time ago and our own experience of socialist construction show that the revolutionary enthusiasm of the people declines after the socialist revolution when they are free of any worries about food, clothing and shelter.

Therefore, after the socialist system has been established, the working-class party and state should intensify educational work and further increase the revolutionary enthusiasm of every member of society.

It is 130 years since Marx published the *Communist Manifesto* in 1848, and 60 years have elapsed since the October Socialist Revolution triumphed in Russia under Lenin's leadership. Over this period great changes have taken place in the international communist movement and the liberation struggle of the oppressed. After World War II in particular the chains of capitalism fell apart and the socialist revolution triumphed in a great number of countries, and many oppressed peoples won national independence, throwing off the colonial fetters of imperialism and they are now advancing along the socialist road.

Many years have passed since Lenin advanced the theory that socialism could triumph in a single country. However, no country has ever attained communism although it is well over half a century since the victory of the socialist revolution in Russia and despite the fact that many countries are now building socialism.

In the *Communist Manifesto* Marx pointed out that the history of every society that had existed hitherto had been a history of class struggle, and advanced the theory of the continuous revolution. Even after it has seized power the working class should continue with the revolution to build socialism and communism. The continuation of the revolution urgently demands education to improve steadily the revolutionary consciousness of the people.

The most complicated and difficult task in building a socialist and communist society is to capture the ideological fortress of communism through the re-education of men. But no one has ever clarified the question of fostering men of a communist type, the question of socialist education, and its model cannot be found in any country. Since no adequate solution has been found to this question, communism has not yet been realized anywhere, although socialism triumphed a long time ago. Communists must draw a serious lesson from this.

Today the move towards socialism is the irresistible trend of the times. The countries of the third world and most of the newly independent nations are now declaring their intention to advance along the road to socialism. True, the socialism advocated by each of them may be different—whether scientific socialism or unscientific socialism. Some people are even claiming now that their socialism is a religious socialism. But whatever kind of socialism they may claim to be adopting, they all recognize that socialism is good.

At present many of the countries that aspire to socialism, including the newly independent nations, are watching how socialism is being built in the countries that are already socialist. For this reason the socialist countries must build socialism better and find a credible solution to the problem of education to supply a model for the other countries that aspire to socialism.

The main task in socialist education is to remould people ideologically and raise their cultural and technical levels. Ideological remoulding, that is, eradicating the feudalist and capitalist ideas that linger in people's minds and educating and nurturing people to be ardent communist revolutionaries, is one of the most important aspects of socialist education.

Ideological remoulding requires, first of all, the strengthening of class education, so that no one is allowed to forget the distressing days of exploitation by the imperialists, landowners and capitalists, and so that everyone wages a resolute struggle against the system of exploitation. In particular, the younger generation should be made to understand clearly how the landowners and capitalists exploited the peasants and workers so that they will hate the system of exploitation implacably.

In order to remould the thinking of everyone we should also intensify education in socialist patriotism. Everyone should be made to fully appreciate the superiority of the socialist system, so that he will treasure it and love it and defend the gains of the revolution to the last against any encroachment of its enemies.

In educating people in communism it is essential to inspire in them revolutionary optimism. Everyone should be encouraged to fight for building a socialist and communist society with an unshakable faith in communism and in the victory of the revolution, to cherish the future and continue to innovate and advance.

The basic aim of ideological education should be to cultivate loyalty to the Party in the people. Unbounded loyalty to the Party is the fundamental quality of a communist. Loyalty to the Party should be displayed by a strong Party spirit, working-class spirit and people-oriented spirit. In other words, it should be expressed in the noble trait of fighting with complete devotion for the Party and the revolution, for the working class and the people. It is only when the people are educated in the spirit of loyalty to the Party that they can devote themselves completely to the struggle for the Party and the revolution, for the working class and the people. However superior a man's cultural and technical knowledge may be, it is useless if he lacks loyalty to the Party. We need people that are not only armed with revolutionary theory and possess a high level of scientific and technical knowledge, but also have a high degree of loyalty to the Party and fight with single-minded devotion for the Party and the revolution, for the working class and the people. In socialist education, therefore, it is necessary to direct primary attention to teaching people to be unfailingly loyal to the Party.

Another important aspect of socialist education is to raise everyone's cultural and technical levels. The struggle to build socialism and communism is a very hard struggle in which every problem has to be solved by independent effort against a capitalist background. So, it is necessary for everyone to adhere closely to an independent stand and display his creative spirit to the full in the revolutionary struggle and the work of construction. For this, everyone should have a high level of cultural and technical knowledge. Only then will it be possible to dispel any illusions about the technology of the developed capitalist countries, do away with the worship of major powers and dogmatism and conduct the revolutionary struggle and the work of construction creatively based on *Juche* in conformity with the actual situation in one's own country. When the cultural and technical levels are low, one will accept the ideas of others mechanically, but if those levels are high, one will be able to display one's creative initiative and solve every problem in the revolutionary struggle and the work of construction by oneself.

In socialist education we should coordinate ideological education and cultural and technical education. In order to build socialism and communism, two fortresses must be captured, namely the ideological and material fortresses. In order to take these two fortresses we should guard against leaning too far towards cultural and technical education while neglecting ideological education, and vice versa. In order to build a socialist and communist society successfully, we should put great efforts into promoting both the ideological remoulding of all the people and the work of raising their cultural and technical levels.

It is of particular importance in socialist education to nurture the younger generation, the successors to the revolutionary cause, to become ardent revolutionaries and communists. Whether or not we do this is of vital importance in preparing the younger generation to take over and accomplish our revolutionary cause.

The revolutionary struggle is a protracted, arduous struggle. Although the aim of the revolution remains unchanged, the generations pass ceaselessly. Our revolutionary task has not been fulfilled and we have not yet reunified our country. We are now conducting the revolutionary struggle and the work of construction in direct confrontation with the American imperialists, the chieftains of imperialism. Half of our country is still occupied by them and south Korea has been turned into a den of reactionaries of every type. As long as the American imperialists and reactionaries remain in south Korea, we cannot ease up in our struggle for a single moment. We must reunify the country and carry the revolution through to the end. It is only when we have educated and trained the successors to the revolution properly that it will be possible to continue the revolution, reunify the country and carry the cause of socialism and communism through to a successful conclusion.

Even in the early days of the anti-Japanese revolutionary struggle we could see that the revolution would be protracted, and paid close attention to the education of the younger generation which would have to advance it further. In the early 1930s we set up the Samgwang School in Guyushu as an experiment, and there we gave free schooling to young people and raised many of them to become revolutionaries through socialist education. Nearly all those who studied at the Samgwang School joined the revolutionary struggle, and even though some of them did not participate in the revolutionary struggle, not one of them took the reactionary road.

Experience has shown us that the proper education of the younger generation, the people who will succeed to the revolutionary cause, is essential for bringing them up to be ardent revolutionaries and communists and for carrying the revolutionary cause through to a successful conclusion. Therefore, we should pay particular attention to their education and bring them up to be ardent revolutionaries and communists. If socialist education is to be successful, party guidance of educational work should be strengthened.

The steady enhancement of the leadership role of the party in the revolution and construction is a sure guarantee for victory in everything that is attempted. We cannot advance towards communism unless we enhance the leadership role of the working-class party and strengthen the socialist state's functions of proletarian dictatorship.

It is a revisionist trait to negate the leadership role of the party in the revolution and construction and the socialist state's functions of the proletarian dictatorship.

Marx said that proletarian dictatorship is essential in the period of transition from capitalism to communism. Lenin defended and adhered to Marx's theory on proletarian dictatorship and advanced the proposition that communism is Soviet power plus electrification.

We should have a proper understanding of the propositions of the Marxist-Leninist classics and uphold and develop them. In Lenin's proposition, Soviet power means the proletarian dictatorship and electrification means carrying out the technical revolution to automate all production processes, not simply the construction of many power stations.

In order to build socialism and communism we should strengthen the proletarian dictatorship and remould the ideological consciousness of the people by enhancing the leadership role of the Party; we should eliminate the distinctions between heavy and light labour, between agricultural and industrial labour and between mental and physical labour through the technical revolution.

In future, too, we should continue to strengthen Party guidance in socialist education to bring up all the pupils and students to be able builders of communism equipped with a wide range of knowledge, noble virtues and a strong physique.

By re-educating everyone in communism through better socialist education, we should lead them to struggle selflessly for the consolidation and development of the socialist system in the northern half of Korea, for the reunification of the country, for the complete defeat of imperialism throughout the world in league with all revolutionary peoples and for the building of a new society free from exploitation and oppression.

We should set the pattern of the socialist educational system in the northern half of Korea to demonstrate the superiority of our socialist system to the people of south Korea.

We should make our working class and all our people thoroughly understand that proper socialist education is essential to further consolidate and develop the socialist system, to safeguard and defend the socialist country, to imbue revolutionary, working-class and communist qualities into all the people and to accelerate more rapidly the socialist and communist cause, and should further strengthen and develop socialist education. With this aim in mind I submit to this plenary meeting of the Central Committee of the Party the *Theses on Socialist Education* compiled on the basis of the rich experience accumulated in the course of conducting socialist education over a long period of time in our country.

I firmly believe that you will take an active part in the debate on the *Theses on Socialist Education,* and strive more vigorously to advance the building of socialism and communism and hasten the cause of national reunification by examining and reviewing your past work and improving the work of socialist education in accordance with the theses.

3

THESES ON SOCIALIST EDUCATION

Kim Il-Sung

Editors' note: *This speech was delivered at the 14th Plenary Meeting of the Fifth Central Committee of the Workers' Party of Korea on September 05, 1977. It is the program that guided the construction of socialist education and that details most comprehensively the pedagogical, philosophical, political, organizational, and overall educational ethos of the project and its connection to socialism and the peaceful reunification of the peninsula.*

The working-class party and state that have seized power are faced with the mighty task of building socialism and communism. It is imperative for building socialism and communism to continue the revolution even after the socialist system has been established and to push ahead with the struggle to capture the ideological and material fortresses of communism.

Of these two fortresses, it is the ideological one that is more important to conquer. It is only when the people, the masters of society, are re-educated in communism that the fundamental question of building communism can be solved and the material fortress taken with success. The working-class party and state should therefore put their first efforts into conquering the ideological fortress by re-educating the people in communism during

THESES ON SOCIALIST EDUCATION 65

the period of transition from capitalism to socialism.

In order to take the ideological fortress of communism, educational work must be well managed. Good education will make it possible to do away with the ideological and cultural backwardness that is a remnant of the old society, to train everyone to be people of a communist type and to promote the revolution and construction.

Education is a decisive factor in the revolution and in determining the fate of the nation. Without education there can be neither social progress nor national prosperity, at any time or in any nation. The question of education acquires still greater importance in those newly independent countries which have won their freedom from imperialist, colonial rule.

Since the earliest days of its leadership of the revolution and construction, our Party has paid close attention to education. At every stage of the revolution our Party has mapped out and put into practice a sound education policy and the Party and state have put a lot of work into education.

Thanks to the wise leadership and sound education policy of our Party, what remained of the education system that had been in force under colonial enslavement was quickly eliminated and an advanced socialist system of education established. And brilliant success has been achieved in public education and in training our own cadres. In our country today universal 11-year education is compulsory and every member of the younger generation studies to the best of his ability at state expense. An army of intellectuals, a whole million strong, has grown up and is now efficiently running the state organs and economic and cultural institutions. Our working people who once lagged far behind modern civilization, are all working as master-builders of socialism and their cultural and technical levels are of middle school standard or higher. A new era of socialist culture has been opened up in this land where total ignorance once prevailed.

Today we are confronted with the momentous task of developing education for socialism in line with the demands of the revolution. The situation today, in which the three revolutions—ideological, technical and cultural—are really getting into their stride, demands urgently that socialist education should be developed further. By accelerating the ideological and cultural revolutions and pressing on with the technical revolution by developing socialist education, we shall bring earlier the victory of the socialist and communist cause.

1. The Fundamental Principle of Socialist Pedagogy

Socialist education is an undertaking to teach people to be independent and creative social beings.

Man can be an independent and creative social being only when he is conscious of his independence and creative ability. Independent consciousness and creative ability are not inherent. No man is born with an ideology or knowledge. It is through education that man acquires independent ideology and a knowledge of nature and society and cultivates the creative ability to understand and change the world.

The aim of socialist education is to bring up people to become communist revolutionaries who have independence and creativity. Socialist education should serve the socialist system and the revolutionary cause of the working class by developing people as communist revolutionaries who fight with devotion for society, for the people and for socialism and communism.

For socialist education to achieve its aims and fulfil its mission, the fundamental principle of socialist pedagogy should be thoroughly applied. The fundamental principle of socialist pedagogy is to make people revolutionary, working-class and communist. In other words, it is to equip people with the revolutionary ideas of communism and, on the basis of this, ensure that they acquire sound scientific knowledge and are in good physical condition.

Revolutionary ideas, sound knowledge and a healthy body are the qualities and qualifications essential for a communist. Only when a man has communist ideas, sound knowledge and a healthy body can he be a true communist revolutionary and play the role of master in the revolution and construction.

Making people revolutionary and working-class is a legitimate demand for building socialism and communism and a basic revolutionary task that confronts the working-class party and state during the period of transition from capitalism to socialism.

Even after the socialist system has been established, outdated ideas persist in the minds of the people for a long time and the ideological and cultural infiltration of imperialism continues. Without making energetic efforts to imbue everyone with revolutionary and working-class qualities it is impossible to root out the old way of thinking that lingers in the minds of the people and to stop imperialist ideological and cultural infiltration. Equipping people with revolutionary, working-class ideas and a communist world outlook through an intensive campaign to imbue everyone with revolutionary and working-class qualities is essential in overcoming the corrosive action of backward ideas and in consolidating and developing the socialist system.

Making people revolutionary and working-class is fundamental to developing communist revolutionaries.

Man is a social being with ideological consciousness. A person's thinking determines his value and quality and regulates all his activities. To remould people is, in essence, to remould their thinking, and what is fundamental to the development of a communist is to arm him with communist ideas. It is only when a person is armed with these ideas that he can acquire the qualities of a communist and display a high degree of independence and creativity.

If a man is to study hard and use his knowledge effectively in the revolution and construction it is essential that he be armed with communist ideas. Only a person who has revolutionary, working-class ideas can ensure that every bit of what he has learned is practical and can devote all his wisdom and talents to the great work of building socialism and communism. Learning that is not based on revolutionary, communist ideas is of no use at all.

Socialist education, therefore, should be the process of the ideological revolution to make people revolutionary and working-class. In socialist education the main emphasis should be laid on ideological education and the main effort should be directed towards arming people with communist ideas. The content and method of socialist education should be geared towards imbuing revolutionary and working-class qualities into people, and all means and facilities of education should tend towards remoulding their thinking.

A communist should possess a sound knowledge of nature and society as well as communist ideas. The acquisition of scientific knowledge is vital to the all-round development of a man and is the basis for establishing his scientific world outlook. The creative activities of man for reforming nature and society should be supported by scientific knowledge. Only when a man has a full knowledge of nature and society as well as communist ideas can he become a fully-developed communist equipped with a revolutionary world outlook and work purposefully in the struggle to remodel nature and society.

In socialist education, importance should be attached to equipping people with a profound knowledge of nature, society and modern technology. The people should be given a systematic knowledge of mankind's achievements in science and engineering and a profound understanding of the world and their power to act to transform it in a revolutionary way should be cultivated in them.

A strong body is the physical basis for intellectual and practical activities. Without a strong body, a man cannot hope to be independent and creative in his activities. Socialist education should make a positive contribution to developing the physical strength of the people.

The thinking, knowledge and physical strength of a man are closely related. Socialist education aimed at bringing up fully-developed communists who are independent and creative, should give both intellectual and physical training in an integrated manner, although priority should be given to ideological training.

In order to carry out socialist education satisfactorily, it is necessary to adhere to the following principles.

First, Party loyalty and working-class loyalty should be embodied in education. Education in a class society always acquires a class character. In its class essence, socialist education is Party and working-class education.

Party loyalty and working-class loyalty are the lifeblood of socialist education and the decisive factor that guarantees success in educational work. Only Party and working-class education can form people into revolutionaries true to the Party and the revolution and contribute to the revolutionary cause of the working class, to the cause of socialism and communism.

The most important factor in developing socialist education into Party and working-class education is to establish our Party's monolithic ideological system in it.

Socialist education must be guided entirely by the revolutionary ideas of the Party. The guiding idea of our socialist education is communism and the *Juche* idea. Communism and the *Juche* idea are the ideological, theoretical and methodological basis of socialist education. Communism and the *Juche* idea provide full answers to all the theoretical and practical problems that arise in education and indicate the direction in which socialist education should progress. Socialist education must be guided by communism and the *Juche* idea, and these must be applied fully in all areas of educational work.

The policy of the Party reflects its intentions and requirements. All educational work must be conducted in accordance with Party policy and teaching, too, must be based on Party policy.

Socialist education must be carried out under the guidance of the Party. Without the leadership of the Party, it is impossible to implement the Party's intentions and political requirements in educational work. By strengthening the Party's leadership we shall eliminate "liberalism" and irregularities from education and establish revolutionary discipline so that all education is conducted in accordance with Party policy.

Establishing the Party's monolithic ideological system in education is aimed at training people to be revolutionaries who are totally loyal to the Party. All the levers of socialist education must be made to serve the training of people to be revolutionary fighters who are loyal to the Party, and education in Party loyalty should be the keynote of the whole educational process.

The work of establishing the Party's monolithic ideological system in education is closely linked with the political and ideological defence of the Party. We must prevent ideological elements that are antagonistic to the Party and unsound inclinations infiltrating this sphere and fight strongly against their slightest manifestation.

In order to develop socialist education into Party and working-class education, it is necessary to give it a working-class edge. To give education a working-class edge means marking a clear definition between the working and the capitalist class and between communism and capitalism in all spheres of education and jealously defending the interests of the working class and meeting its every need.

The class struggle is continuing in socialist society. If we fail to give a sharp working-class edge to education and give a patchy education which obscures distinctions between the working and the capitalist class, people may acquire a patchy outlook and so may society. In education the working-class party and state must always stand by their class position and revolutionary principles and solve all theoretical and practical problems that arise in education in accordance with the interests and needs of the working class.

In order to defend the interests and meet the needs of the working class in education, a campaign should be launched to combat all non-working-class elements. We must completely eliminate what remains of feudalism and capitalism in every sphere of education, so that socialist education develops in harmony with the character of socialist society and with working-class aspirations. We must prevent any reactionary bourgeois ideas and degenerate habits spread by imperialists and their minions from infiltrating education and in particular we must be on our guard against bourgeois theories of education. We must continue to fight relentlessly against all opportunist ideological trends including revisionist theories that negate the Party and working-class character of education and preach the non-ideological character and "liberalization" of education. Thus, we will safeguard the Party and working-class character of socialist education and ensure its purity in our country.

Secondly, Juche must be established in education. Socialism and communism is built with the national state as a unit and with the people of each nation as the masters of the revolution and construction. The environment and conditions in each country are different, as are the revolutionary tasks that have to be done. Therefore, socialist education must become *Juche*-oriented education that makes teaching and training conform with the realities of each country and the interests of the people there and trains the people to be the masters of the revolution in their own country.

An important factor in establishing *Juche* in education is to find a creative solution to all the problems that arise by adopting an independent stand. Socialist education is creative work to develop the people who live and act in specific conditions. There can never be an educational theory or experience that can be applied uniformly to the specific circumstances and conditions in every country. We must solve all the problems of theory and practice that arise in education creatively by our own efforts in accordance with the situation in our country and in the interests of the Korean revolution.

In order to establish *Juche* in education, the main emphasis in instruction should be placed on the things of one's own country and people should be taught to understand their national things.

Koreans should conduct the revolution in Korea and build socialism and communism in Korea. If Koreans want to play their part to the full as masters of the Korean revolution and take responsibility for the revolution and construction in their own country, they must know all about Korea past and present and about the Korean revolution. Through education our people must become immersed in our Party policy and brilliant revolutionary traditions and become acquainted with the history, culture, geography and natural conditions of our country. It is only when our people know about their own country and revolution that they are in a position to solve the difficult problems that arise in the revolution and construction by making good use of the country's full potential and to fight selflessly for our revolutionary cause with the pride of working for the Korean revolution under our Party's leadership and with love for the country and the people.

As for science and technology from abroad, they should be taught from a *Juche* standpoint and adapted to the conditions and actual situation in our country. If we fail to adopt even advanced science and technology critically to suit our actual situation, they will actually have an adverse effect on our revolution and construction rather than benefit them. The purpose of learning and introducing things from abroad should always be to gain a better understanding of our own things and to carry out our revolution and construction more efficiently.

We should reject sycophancy towards major powers and dogmatism in education. If such things are tolerated in education, all kinds of opportunist and reactionary educational theories and ideologies may find their way in and it will become impossible to develop education in the interests of our revolution and our people. We should categorically repudiate sycophancy and dogmatism and develop socialist education into a *Juche*-oriented, revolutionary education.

Thirdly, education should be combined with revolutionary practice. Education is born of practical needs and serves practice. Only when it is linked with practice can education fulfil its mission. Socialist education should be integrated with revolutionary working-class activities for socialism and communism. Only then can it contribute to the socialist and communist cause.

The combination of education and revolutionary practice is indispensable in bringing people up to be communist revolutionaries equipped with living knowledge and practical ability.

Practice is the starting point of understanding, the criterion of truth and the motive power for the development of theory. Revolutionary practice helps people cultivate their practical skills and tempers them for the revolution. It is by acquiring a knowledge of the world as well as practical skills that man becomes the most powerful being in the world.

It is only when education is closely linked with revolutionary practice that every bit of knowledge imparted can be useful in the revolution and construction; that it can train people as socialist and communist builders with living knowledge and practical skills. Theory for theory's sake and knowledge for knowledge's sake that are detached from revolutionary practice are utterly useless in our society. In socialist education universal principles and theories should be taught to the students in close combination with practice, and education should be conducted in such a way that all theories and knowledge can contribute to dealing with the problems that arise in the revolution and construction.

Education should always be kept in close touch with reality. Education should be sensitive to the vibrant realities of our country and all aspects of education, including its content and methods, should be improved and perfected in accordance with developing reality.

Fourthly, the socialist state should take the responsibility for organizing and conducting education. Socialist education is an instrument of the socialist state for training the people ideologically and culturally. Through educational work the socialist state functions as a cultural educator. The socialist state should be responsible for educational work in order to accelerate communist education and training and hasten the victory of the socialist and communist cause.

The socialist state should keep education well in advance of all other work. Socialist education is work with the people to develop them as communists. Giving priority to remoulding people, to working with people, is a sure guarantee for success in all our work.

The revolution and construction should begin with the education of people. The socialist state should always attach primary importance to education in the revolutionary struggle and construction work and adhere to the revolutionary stand of solving all problems through effective education.

The socialist state should run education on the principle of the continuous education of all members of society.

Socialist education is people-oriented education to serve the working masses. It should contribute to educating every member of society continuously so that everyone is brought up as a communist who has independence and creativity.

The continuous education of all members of society is indispensable for building socialism and communism. Only by educating all members of society continually can any differences in the ideological, technical and cultural standards of people be eliminated and the aim of making our whole society working-class, revolutionary and intellectual be achieved.

The socialist state should establish an advanced system and a rational programme for the uninterrupted education of every member of society and push ahead with educating both the younger generation and adults as well as training its own cadres.

The socialist state should take the responsibility for providing suitable educational conditions. In socialist society, where the means of production are owned by the state and society and educational institutions are directed by the state, educational work can only be successful when the state looks after it in a responsible manner.

For the socialist state, which serves the people, to provide suitable conditions in which to educate the people is an honourable duty. The socialist state should take full responsibility for doing everything that is needed for education–training teachers, building schools, providing educational facilities, teaching aids and tools and school fixtures and fittings.

2. The Content of Socialist Education

The content of education determines both its quality and nature. The content of socialist education should be such that it will make the people revolutionary and working-class and bring them up as communists who are mentally, morally and physically prepared and fully developed. The content of socialist education should be fully revolutionary, scientific and realistic.

1) Political and Ideological Education

Political and ideological education is the most important aspect of socialist education. It is only through proper political and ideological education that it is possible to train students to be revolutionaries who are equipped with a revolutionary outlook on the world and the ideological and moral qualities of a communist. And only when it is based on sound political and ideological education will the people's scientific, technological and physical education be successful.

It is of paramount importance in political and ideological education to arm the students fully with the *Juche* idea. The *Juche* idea provides a scientific and revolutionary view of the world that is indispensable for communists. Students will only become true masters of the revolution and construction and independent and creative revolutionary workers when they are fully armed with the *Juche* idea.

In socialist education primary attention should be paid to teaching the students the *Juche* idea, and everything should be subordinated to this. In order to arm the students with the Juche idea, education in Party policy and revolutionary traditions should be improved.

All our Party's policies proceed from and embody the *Juche* idea. Party policy should be taught to the students systematically and in full so that they all gain a clear understanding of its essence and its correctness and have firm faith in it.

The brilliant revolutionary traditions of our Party have the rich ideological content required to arm people with the *Juche* idea, to make them revolutionary and have a great influence upon them. Through more intensive education in these revolutionary traditions, we should make the students aware of the historical roots of our Party and revolution and make them able to understand fully the ideological system of *Juche*, our immortal revolutionary achievements, our valuable fighting experience, and our revolutionary method and popular style of work acquired during the anti-Japanese revolutionary struggle.

In teaching Party policy and revolutionary traditions, the main emphasis should be placed on cultivating loyalty to the Party. All children and students will thus be moulded into revolutionary fighters who are unfailingly loyal to the Party, fully imbued with our Party's revolutionary ideas and prepared to support and defend the Party resolutely and rally closely around it to carry out its policies without question.

Next in importance in political and ideological education is to intensify revolutionary, communist education so as to equip the students fully with the revolutionary consciousness of the working class and with communist morality.

Faith in communism and revolutionary optimism are high moral qualities of revolutionaries who fight for communism. The justice of the communist cause, the inevitability of victory and the bright prospects for communism should be clearly understood by students, so that they hold a firm belief in the victory of communism and fight for it with devotion. The students should be taught to be optimistic and hold fast to the idea of the continuous revolution.

The kernel of communist ideology is the class consciousness of the working class, and the main content of communist education is class education. By intensifying class education, we should make sure that all the students fight selflessly for the interests of the working class with an unwavering working-class viewpoint and on a firm working-class stand. It is particularly important to educate them to hate the enemies of the revolution. Those who do not hate the enemies of the revolution cannot fight with determination against them nor can they become true revolutionaries. By bringing the students to hate imperialism and the landowner and capitalist classes, we should make certain that they fight resolutely against both our class enemies and the system of exploitation.

Collectivism is the basis of social life under socialism and communism and a principle that guides the actions of communists. We should educate all the students to outgrow individualism and selfishness, and to work, study and live according to the collectivist principle of "One for all and all for one", and fight with devotion for society and the people, for the interests of the Party and the revolution.

A love of work is a salient characteristic of the communist.

All students should be taught to regard work as honourable and sacred, to enjoy work, to observe labour discipline willingly and to participate conscientiously in any common endeavour for the good of the collective and society.

Education in socialist patriotism should be improved. Socialist patriotism is the spirit of loving the socialist homeland with the working-class state power, socialist system, independent national economy, and brilliant national culture. All students should be encouraged to be proud of their nation, have a deep love of their country and people, cherish their fine national heritage and traditions and be willing to sacrifice themselves in the fight for the prosperity and progress of the socialist homeland. Students should be taught to take loving care of their desks and chairs and, further, to treasure all communal property of the state and society and manage the nation's economic life carefully and assiduously.

Students should be armed with proletarian internationalism. All our students should be educated to offer active support for the revolutionary struggle of the peoples of the world for peace, democracy, national independence, and socialism, to strengthen friendship and solidarity with them and to fight staunchly for victory in the world revolution.

Children and students should be taught to abide by the letter and spirit of socialist law. Socialist law is the rule of action and the principle of life which everyone in socialist society is bound to observe, by displaying a high degree of political consciousness. All students should be taught to respect the state law and observe it voluntarily and to wage a principled struggle against any violations of law and order.

Children and students should be taught to acquire communist morality and to adhere to the socialist way of life. All students should be made to rid themselves completely of any outdated moral concepts and conventions, to abide by communist moral standards willingly and to live revolutionary lives consonant with the socialist way of life.

The process by which a man's ideological consciousness develops is closely related to the process by which he grows. Therefore, political and ideological education should be stepped up gradually from an early age, from the lowest to the most advanced stage of education. Kindergarten education should start with giving the children a general idea of social phenomena and giving them the beginnings of political and ideological awareness, and as they grow older and education proceeds to a higher level, ideological education should be intensified and the standard of education raised gradually to give them a deep understanding of the essence and fundamentals of social phenomena.

2) Scientific and Technical Education

Scientific and technical education is aimed at making the students aware of the advances in science and technology achieved by mankind and at developing their ability to make use of them. Such education should provide general and specialized knowledge.

The first task is to provide a good general education. General knowledge is indispensable to any member of a socialist society. A good general education at school is essential for enabling the students to gain a wide range of knowledge of nature and society and for building sound foundations for learning modern science and technology in the fields of their specialty. A complete general secondary education is provided through the system of universal 11-year compulsory education in our country.

Instruction in basic knowledge is important in general education. The main emphasis in primary and general secondary education should be placed on teaching the pupils the general concepts and essence of things and phenomena as well as the rudiments of the laws of their change and development, and especially on providing them with a general knowledge of elementary sciences such as mathematics, physics, chemistry and biology.

The rudiments of engineering should also be taught. The students should be introduced to the fundamental principles of production and technology and given an understanding of electricity and machinery and other basic technical knowledge. In general secondary education all students should be encouraged to study at least one form of technology related to our modern industry.

In socialist education it is as wrong to divorce students from production processes by giving general basic knowledge alone at the expense of technical education, as it is to turn general secondary education into vocational training by over-emphasizing technical education at the expense of a basic general education. General secondary education must not fail in its duty to provide a sound basic general knowledge in proper combination with the teaching of basic techniques.

Good education in the arts is necessary during general education. In primary and secondary schools, the teaching of arts subjects should be improved so that all pupils gain a basic knowledge that will enable them to appreciate and be creative in literature and art and so that they develop the ability to play at least one musical instrument and cultivate their aesthetic feelings.

Next comes good, specialized education. This education should be given during higher education after a full general secondary education. It is only by improving specialized education that it is possible to train able technicians and specialists and to realize the aim of making every member of society an intellectual.

Specialized education in natural sciences is required to acquaint the students with the basic principles and theories of the natural sciences and the latest breakthroughs in this field, and to give them adequate knowledge for solving any new scientific and technical problems that arise in their revolutionary activities.

Specialized education in social sciences is required to provide the students with a full understanding of the objective laws of social progress, the theories of class struggle and the strategy and tactics of the revolution. It should also make them aware of the valuable successes and experience gained by our Party in solving difficult problems in a unique way in every area of politics, the economy and culture. Likewise, the ability should be nurtured in the students to give sound theoretical explanations and publicity to Party policy and to offer a correct scientific clarification of the theoretical and practical problems arising in the revolution and construction.

In specialized technical education, modern technology should be taught. The students should be fully introduced to the principles of modern production and engineering and should acquire specialized knowledge of some aspects of technology. They should also be trained to master the skills of handling automated installations and other modern equipment.

The content of scientific and technical education should be continually supplemented and enriched in accordance with the demands of real life and based on the latest breakthroughs in science and engineering.

Scientific and technical education should be wholly keyed to Party policy. Instruction in all subjects should be based entirely on Party policy and linked to the situation in our country. We should thus make sure that the students learn things that are necessary for our revolution and apply their knowledge and skills in their revolutionary activities.

3) Physical Education

The aim of physical education is to develop the bodies of children and students and prepare them fully for both work and national defence.

That the children and young people have strong bodies is essential for the revolutionary struggle and for building a powerful and prosperous society. Their strong bodies developed through effective physical training will provide greater energy in the work to promote the revolution and construction and will increase the strength of the nation.

Physical education is of importance not only because it increases the physical strength of the children and young people but also because it tempers their minds and wills and raises the level of their culture. Through sporting activities the children and students cultivate courage, audacity, fortitude and perseverance and increase their sporting skills and cultural attainments.

All educational institutions should offer the students sufficient physical training. This education should be improved particularly at primary and secondary schools that are bringing the children up at the time of their most rapid physical growth.

Physical training at school should centre on strengthening the children's bodies and making them physically well-proportioned. It should accord with the natural and geographical features of our country, the physical characteristics of our people, the sexes and ages of the children and students and the physiological requirements of their bodies.

Physical education which helps to increase the stature of the children and students and develop their physiques harmoniously should be systematic, and physical training for national defence should also be promoted.

Physical education and sport should be encouraged and made an everyday activity of the masses. At school, collective physical education and sporting activities in which the vast majority take part should be held regularly.

There should be many out-of-school sporting activities for the students. A wide variety of physical education and sporting activities, including exercises during break, group running, mass games and athletics meetings, should be arranged and various sporting circle activities should be conducted at school, so that all the students are strengthening their bodies all the time and become skilled in at least one type of sport.

3. The Methods of Socialist Education

Socialist education can only be successful if scientific and revolutionary methods are employed. We should adopt scientific and revolutionary methods of educating in line with the objectives and mission of socialist education and run education according to these methods.

1) Heuristic Teaching

The main form of school education is teaching, and the basic method of teaching is heuristics. This method enables the students to gain a proper understanding of what they have been taught, so that the aims of education are achieved.

Heuristic teaching is an extremely good method that ties in well with socialist education and the laws of cognition.

By its nature, socialist education demands methods of teaching that encourage independence and creativity. Heuristics give students an understanding of the content of what they are being taught by encouraging them to think positively and so are a great help to increasing their independence and creativity.

The subject of cognition is man. Only through his own positive thinking can man recognize the essential nature of things and phenomena. The heuristic method of teaching stimulates the minds of the students and helps them to identify the essence of things and phenomena readily.

In our schools the teaching of all subjects should be done by heuristic methods. In heuristic instruction various teaching methods should be applied to suit the students' preparedness and characteristics, on the basis of building up their self-awareness and a positive attitude and guaranteeing the logic, system and sequence of the content of the lessons.

An important aspect of heuristics is to provide an illuminating explanation through lectures and conversation. Explanation should be vivid, convincing and extremely logical so that the students can readily understand what they are taught.

In order to fully develop the students' ability to think, there should be a great deal of discussion and debate and question and answer sessions should be conducted. This is our Party's traditional teaching method and it has been tried and tested and proved to be efficient. The introduction of this method will enable the students to gain an extensive and profound understanding of what they are taught.

Visual aids and demonstration play an important part in giving the students a vivid understanding of things and phenomena and of scientific principles and in developing their own thinking. At school the content of lessons should be envisaged to suit the characteristics of the subject and a variety of modern visual aids should be used widely so that visual and demonstrative education is improved.

The ideological education of students should be conducted through explanation and persuasion. It is only when the students themselves understand and accept communist ideology that it can become a firm belief. Therefore, ideological education should be neither coercive nor even crammed, but always conducted by explanation and persuasion, so that the students understand and sympathize with advanced ideas of their own accord. Delinquents and laggards, too, should be treated kindly by persuasion, so that they come to identify and correct their defects and shortcomings by themselves.

Explanation and persuasion should be conducted tirelessly and perseveringly to suit the character and preparedness of each student.

Another fundamental method of ideological education is to influence the students by positive examples. Good examples are an active criticism of the negative and a clear demonstration to people of how they should work and live. They are therefore a powerful driving force in overcoming negative influences on the people and encouraging new and progressive ideas.

Children and young people are sensitive to new things, have a strong sense of justice and like to follow the example of others. So positive examples can arouse great sympathy in children and students and be widely accepted.

The heroic struggle waged by our anti-Japanese revolutionary fighters of the past is an example that teaches the truth of real life and struggle to the younger generation who have not experienced the ordeals of the revolution. Schools should make great efforts to educate the students by referring to the shining examples set by our anti-Japanese revolutionary fighters of the past.

The good examples set by other students exert a tremendous influence, because they are connected directly with their own life. Any positive example set should be noted immediately and drawn on widely so that other students act on it in their studies and life. Meanwhile, their own positive qualities should be actively encouraged and developed so that they can overcome their negative characteristics by themselves.

2) COMBINING THEORETICAL EDUCATION WITH PRACTICAL TRAINING, AND EDUCATION WITH PRODUCTIVE LABOUR

Combining theoretical education with practical training is an important means of educating students to be communist revolutionaries equipped with useful, living knowledge. Theories obtained from books only become working knowledge applicable to revolutionary practice when their truth is substantiated in practice and when they are combined with an ability to apply them.

In school, the lessons and lectures should be properly combined with experiments and practical activities, so that the students digest what they have learned in class and develop the ability to apply it in practice. In education it is particularly important to give the students effective practical training through productive work and in their own specialty. Training through production at secondary school should be conducted with a view to encouraging the students to acquire a basic knowledge of modern production techniques as well as technical skills for handling tools and machinery. Production and specialty training during higher education should be conducted with stress laid on encouraging the students to master scientific principles and modern technical skills in their own specialty.

There should be more practical work in those subjects that require skill and dexterity. Practice should be based on scientific theories and principles and conducted systematically and in due order so as to increase the independence of the students.

For the students to acquire a living, comprehensive knowledge of the real world, visits to revolutionary battlefields and places connected with our revolutionary history should be planned and arranged and there should be regular visits to public, cultural and educational establishments, factories and other enterprises and cooperative farms.

Education and productive labour should be properly combined. Production work, which is the most important form of social practice, is a powerful way of transforming nature, developing society and educating and remoulding people. Through productive labour man understands and harnesses nature and society and transforms himself and his own ideological consciousness. Participation in productive labour by the students engaged in academic pursuits is very important for them to acquire revolutionary and working-class characteristics and also for improving the quality of education. Through productive labour the students are tempered ideologically, learn the revolutionary loyalty and organization of the working class, consolidate the knowledge they have gained at college and cultivate their ability to put it into practice, accumulate experience in real-life situations and develop their skills.

The requirements of pedagogy should be fully met in leading the students into productive labour. We must guard against both the tendency to neglect productive labour while leaning only on classwork and the tendency to give students an excessive amount of production work. The productive labour of students should be organized rationally so that it is conducive to their education and training.

3) The Development of an Organizational Way of Life and of Social and Political Activities

In order to train children and students politically and ideologically and educate them in a revolutionary way, their organizational way of life and their social and political activities must be developed and combined closely with their classwork.

The organization is a forge for ideological training and a school for revolutionary education. During their time in the Children's Union and the League of Socialist Working Youth, children and students receive ideological education and revolutionary training and cultivate their sense of organization and discipline. It is only through belonging to a revolutionary organization that communist revolutionaries equipped with a noble ideology and a strong sense of organization will be developed.

It is important in developing the organizational life of the students that the children and students participate willingly in the activities of the organization, with a sound attitude towards it. Life in an organization is inevitably a form of political life and a process of maintaining political integrity. Children and students must regard their participation in the organizational activities of the CU and LSWY as a great honour and a sacred duty, and must willingly and conscientiously carry out the assignments and obligations under the rules of their respective organizations.

In the CU and LSWY there should be more criticism, while

the main stress is laid on ideological education. Only an organizational life in an atmosphere of criticism can train the students politically and ideologically and provide them with revolutionary education and contribute to bringing up communist revolutionaries. Criticism and self-criticism must be encouraged among the students and, especially, meetings to review their organizational activities must be conducted at a high political and ideological level.

To develop the students' organizational life, the function and role of CU and LSWY organizations at schools should be increased. These organizations are political guardians who protect the students' political integrity and are also their kind educators. They must make great efforts to protect and control the students' political integrity and to educate and train them politically and ideologically. They should give the students assignments in accordance with their age, preparedness and psychological characteristics and help them to carry them out properly; they should also regularly review how their assignments have been carried out and give them new ones, so that every student is always kept busy.

It is important to encourage the students to take part in a lot of social and political activities. Social and political activity is a practical way for the students to apply what they have learned at school to actual situations; it is a revolutionary activity that makes a direct contribution to building socialism. By drawing the students into a variety of social and political activities, we shall train them from their early years to be true masters of society dedicated to the struggle to improve society and the lives of the people, to be competent social and political activists who can educate, organize and mobilize the masses.

The students should be made to form information teams, such as Party-policy information teams, scientific information teams, and hygiene information teams, to explain Party policy to the masses and spread scientific and technical knowledge as well as information on culture and hygiene. We should also encourage them to step up the activities of the hygiene guards and greenery guards, as well as various other good conduct campaigns such as the campaign to create CU and LSWY groves and the campaign to help build socialism.

It is particularly important to encourage the university students to take an active part in the three-revolution team movement in their social and political activities. Their participation in this movement should be planned, so that they will play an active part in the ideological, technical and cultural revolutions and, at the same time, temper themselves politically and ideologically.

4) THE COMBINATION OF SCHOOL AND SOCIAL EDUCATION

While receiving organizational and systematic education at school, the students are at the same time educated through their life in society. Therefore, in order to educate the younger generation properly, we should, while improving school education, educate the students correctly wherever they are subject to educational influences, and closely link school and social education.

The combination of these two forms of education is the main characteristic and advantage of socialist education that stems from the nature of the socialist system. In socialist society where solidarity and cooperation among the working people is the basis of social relations and collectivism is the basis of social life, school and society have a common goal and interests with regard to the education of the younger generation. By sharing common aims and interests, a sure guarantee is provided for making the education of the younger generation the work of the whole of society, and for forging close links between school and social education.

If we are to link school and social education properly, we should promote social education, but still ensure that school education plays the decisive role.

In socialist society social education plays an important role in developing the students as communists. Social education makes an important contribution to educating the students politically and ideologically and giving them an understanding of science and engineering, literature and the arts and sporting techniques. We should handle social education properly in order to strengthen school education and consolidate and supplement its achievements.

An important aspect of improving the social education of the students is to increase the responsibility and role played by social educational institutions and make good use of social educational facilities and the means of information and educational work.

Social educational facilities such as the students and children's palaces, students and children's halls. Children's Union camps and libraries are reliable centres for the education of students. We should use these facilities to hold regular political and current affairs lectures, scientific seminars and public discussions and start up various group activities on a wide scale.

Schools and social educational institutions must strengthen their ties, and the teachers and staff of these institutions must work closely together in the education of students. They must regularly discuss any problems arising in the education of students and exchange notes and keep in touch with each other concerning how they educate the students. The home is a cell of society. The educational influence of the home on children and young people is considerable. We must see to it that their homes are revolutionary and that the socialist way of life is thoroughly established there, so that the revolutionary influence of the home is strong. Parents must be exemplary in social and political life and in building socialism, and always be frugal and courteous, so that their every word and action will be instructive and copied by their sons and daughters.

The social environment has a major educational influence on

the children and young people. The content of broadcasts, the press and films must always be revolutionary and a wholesome way of life must be fully established throughout the whole of society, so that everything the students see and hear in society is instructive.

5) CONTINUITY IN PRESCHOOL, SCHOOL AND ADULT EDUCATION

Socialist education must become an all-round, continuous process that educates all the members of society throughout their lives, from the cradle to the grave.

The mind and quality of a man are formed from the cradle, and consolidated and developed throughout his life. Man's understanding of the world grows deeper as the days go by and mankind's knowledge and experience are continually being enriched. In order to train every member of society as a communist equipped with a revolutionary world outlook and sound scientific and technical knowledge, it is essential to educate everyone without interruption from childhood through to old age.

The proper way of educating all members of society throughout their lives is to combine and provide continuity to preschool, school and adult education.

Preschool, school and adult education are successive stages of education which correspond to the stages of growth, and make up a continuous educational process. Preschool education is the first period of human education. Since a person's ideology is formed and his intellectual faculties are developed from early childhood, it is important to give him proper education and implant good habits in him at a tender age.

In preschool education the main stress should be placed on laying the foundations for school education. At kindergarten, while emphasizing revolutionary ideological and moral education, the children should be given proper education according to their mental development, and careful attention should be paid to raising their cultural levels and strengthening them physically. It is particularly important to give a year of compulsory preschool education of a high level of quality in order to prepare the children properly for school.

Kindergarten education should be matched to the psychology of the children through a proper combination of various forms and methods such as lessons using visual aids and demonstration and teaching by songs, dances and games.

At school, one is educated during the most important period of one's life. It is in one's childhood and youth days that one's outlook is formed and that inquiry and cognition are most active while the body is developing fast. Therefore, school education has a decisive bearing on the establishment of a person's outlook and the formation of his personality.

The fundamental task of school education is to bring up all the members of the younger generation to be revolutionaries armed with a revolutionary world outlook and a knowledge of modern science and technology. Through secondary school education the young people should be moulded into men with the broad basis of a revolutionary outlook and good general knowledge of a secondary school standard, while in higher education, training should be provided to make them revolutionary workers who are fully equipped with a revolutionary world outlook and well-versed in modern science and technology.

Adult education is the education of the working people who are actually engaged in socialist construction. It is of great significance in consolidating and developing their revolutionary world outlook and continually raising their level of general knowledge and technical and cultural standards.

A man's ideological consciousness is not immutable; it can change according to the conditions and environment. Science and technology do not stand still, they are advancing all the time. Even those who, at school, have established a revolutionary outlook and reached a high scientific and technological level, cannot consolidate and develop their revolutionary world outlook and cannot keep abreast of the developing situation, unless they continue to receive education. Therefore, adult education should be promoted to consolidate and develop what was achieved during school education and to continue to raise cultural and technical standards to conform with the latest developments.

Adult education deals with working people whose level of general knowledge and technical and cultural standards vary. In our country today adult education embraces those who were unable to receive regular schooling in the past but have attained approximately the educational level of the middle-school leaver through the adult education programme and those who have received secondary education at regular schools, up to and including university graduates.

In order to improve adult education it is necessary to set up a variety of adult education centres to suit the specific needs of the working people of different intellectual levels, so that all of them can study in educational institutions that suit their level.

Close attention should also be paid to educating cadres to meet the demands of the developing situation. While passing them through various refresher courses according to a plan, we should make sure that they attend Saturday studies and Wednesday lectures without fail and put in two hours' regular study every day.

We must see that under the slogan of "The Party, the people and the army must all study!" a revolutionary habit of study is established throughout the whole nation and that every member of society, young and old, studies and studies hard.

4. The Socialist Education System in our Country

Socialist education can only be successful when it is based on an advanced system of education that accords with the nature of socialist society. The socialist education system in our country constitutes a basic guarantee for applying the fundamental principles of socialist pedagogy in education and achieving the objective of socialist education.

The historical roots of our socialist education system were struck during the anti-Japanese revolutionary struggle. In those days, we set out a revolutionary education policy based on the *Juche* idea and, in pursuance of this, used unique methods in conducting educational work. In the course of this, we gained valuable experience in training revolutionaries and established our Party's glorious traditions of revolutionary education. The new system of education created during the anti-Japanese revolutionary struggle is the prototype for our country's socialist education system.

After liberation, in the period of the anti-imperialist, anti-feudal democratic revolution, we abolished the Japanese imperialist colonial enslavement education and set up a people-oriented, democratic education system, as part of the social and economic reforms for building a new country. The democratic education system was further consolidated as the revolution and construction progressed and it gradually developed into a socialist education system. Upon completion of the socialist revolution and with the full-scale promotion of socialist construction, the system, content and method of education were adjusted to suit the requirements of socialist society and so the socialist education system became fully established.

Our socialist education system is a revolutionary system which serves the revolutionary cause of the working class, the cause of building socialism and communism; it is a most people-oriented education system under which the state bears full responsibility for providing everyone with the opportunity to learn.

We should further consolidate, develop and perfect our socialist education system, the advantages and vitality of which have now been proved beyond dispute.

1) THE SYSTEM OF UNIVERSAL COMPULSORY EDUCATION

The socialist education system is essentially universal and compulsory. Socialist education is education for everyone that is aimed at training not just a small section of society but all its members as communists. In our society everyone has the right to be educated and is obliged to study. Our Party and state's education policy, such as the education system, the distribution of educational institutions and the introduction of free education, is based entirely on the principle of education for all.

The fundamental aspect of compulsory education is schooling. Within a short time after liberation, we set up a large number of schools of all levels ranging from primary schools to colleges and universities and established a well-regulated democratic education system and, on this basis, introduced universal compulsory education stage by stage as the revolution and construction advanced and the country's economic foundations were consolidated. Universal compulsory primary education was introduced in 1956, compulsory secondary education in 1958 and then nine-year compulsory technical education in 1967. Since 1972 compulsory 11-year education has been in force, and this is made up of one year of compulsory preschool education and ten years of compulsory education at school.

Universal 11-year education is compulsory and free, and it provides a complete general secondary education to all members of the younger generation up until they reach a working age. It is based on a scientific system of education and is the most thoroughgoing free education, combining a high level of general and technical education.

Our Party pursues the policy of making it compulsory for all the working people to study under some kind of education system, while giving full-term compulsory education to the younger generation at regular schools.

Our Party has established various systems of study-while-you-work alongside the regular education system, and run those systems with success to ensure that not only the children of school age but all the working people without exception study. In accordance with the wise policy of the Party all the working people, including the adults who were denied access to learning in the old exploiter society, can now be educated systematically, and everyone has attained the cultural and technical standards of a middle-school leaver or above. In our country today, under the guidance of the Party and the state, all the working people make it a rule to study to improve their cultural and technical, political and theoretical levels.

The system of universal compulsory education should be further developed and perfected in keeping with the inevitable demands of building socialism and communism. To make this system complete, compulsory higher education should be introduced in the future on the basis of consolidating even further the system of universal 11-year education now in force.

In order to eliminate the distinctions between mental and physical labour and build a communist society, it is necessary to considerably improve the cultural and technical levels of all members of society and make everyone an intellectual. Making the whole society intellectual can only be achieved when everyone in society studies at some kind of institution of higher education. For this, higher education, too, should be made compulsory. It is only by making higher education compulsory that the system of universal compulsory education, as a socialist education system, will become complete.

For the present we should make preparations for the introduction of compulsory higher education at the same time as striving to make a success of universal 11-year compulsory education. And at some time in the future, we should make a big increase to the number of institutions of higher education and gradually move towards the introduction of compulsory higher education. In expanding the system of higher education, the main accent should be on the expansion and development of the study-while-you-work system. Then we should ensure that higher education is given to all the young people once they have completed their 11-year education, without adversely affecting the labour efforts in socialist construction.

In order to make universal education more successful, the educational institutions should be distributed rationally over the regions. This is of great significance in promoting the ideological, technical and cultural revolutions nationwide, reducing the distinctions between town and country areas and developing all the regions in a balanced way.

Educational institutions should be rationally distributed between urban and rural communities and between industrial and agricultural zones by considering the regional characteristics and the general balance. Institutions of higher education should be distributed on the principle of meeting state demands for cadres and setting up a comprehensive training base in every province.

It is important to arrange the composition of the system of higher education rationally according to the sciences. On the basis of an accurate calculation of state demands for cadres at any given moment, universities and colleges and faculties and courses should be established by the sciences, and the size of student intake determined accurately. In particular, with the progress of socialist and communist construction and the great development of natural science and technology, the share of natural science and engineering should be markedly greater than that of the liberal arts.

2) THE SYSTEM OF UNIVERSAL FREE EDUCATION

Compulsory education can only become a reality when it is free. Compulsory education that is not free is never compulsory in practice. The fundamental distinction between the compulsory education in socialist society and the so-called "compulsory education" in capitalist society lies in the fact that education costs are borne by the socialist state, which actually provides the people with the right and freedom to study. State-financed universal free education is possible only in socialist society where the means of production and educational facilities are owned by the state and the people and the interests of the state and the people in education coincide with each other.

The most comprehensive free education is ensured in our country on the principle that the state takes full responsibility for educating the people.

Immediately after liberation, even though our country's economy was in severe difficulties, we took measures to exempt the children of poor families from school fees and provide the students at specialized schools and universities with state grants. In the postwar years universal compulsory primary education and universal compulsory secondary education became free. In 1959 state-financed universal free education was introduced at all the educational institutions in our country.

Now we offer universal 11-year compulsory education entirely free of charge and give free education to all the children and students who study at educational institutions of all levels from kindergartens to institutions of higher learning. Not only school education but also all forms of social education are free, and adult education for cadres and working people is also given at state expense. The proportion of our budget devoted to education is very high, and is increasing every year.

Our system of state-financed universal free education is fully guaranteed by the people-oriented policy of our Party and state which stint nothing for the education of the younger generation and the training of cadres and also by our ever-expanding independent economy.

With the development of education and the consolidation

of the country's economy, the state should improve the educational institutions and facilities, supply all pupils and students with free textbooks and school equipment and even bear the cost of the students' collective hostel life.

3) THE STUDY-WHILE-YOU-WORK SYSTEM

The study-while-you-work system is a superior education system which enables working people in the different areas of socialist construction to study at some educational institution while they continue with their productive activities, their own duties.

Besides the regular system of education, our Party has set up a system of part-time education on the principle of providing education not only for the younger generation but also for the workers, peasants and other sections of the working people, in fact everyone without exception, and has steadily developed it to meet our present needs. Today, this system of education takes such forms as working people's senior middle schools, factory higher specialized schools, factory colleges, correspondence and evening courses and the regular system of study for officials and working people.

This education system makes it possible for the working people to continue studying without leaving their posts in socialist construction, which makes a success of education for all.

The regular education system on its own is not enough to provide education for all, since there are working people who never had the opportunity to learn in the old exploiter society; the regular education system is limited in its scale and length, and educational work and socialist construction need to move ahead simultaneously. The study-while-you-work system of education, along with the normal education system, provides an opportunity for all our people to learn and makes it possible to give continuous schooling to everyone while pushing ahead with socialist construction. In our country today there is no one who is not educated and nobody abandons his studies half-finished; everyone continues studying throughout his life. Herein the correctness of our Party's education policy of developing the full-time and the part-time systems of education simultaneously can be identified, and one of the great advantages of the part-time system of education is also evident.

The study-while-you-work system makes it possible to train large numbers of able officials equipped with a firm revolutionary world outlook and well-versed in theory and practice, and it closely combines education with socialist construction.

Those studying under the part-time education system are student-producers and working officials. Mainly engaged in practical activities, they study theory in compliance with the urgent needs of revolutionary practice, and then apply the theory they have learned to the practice of socialist construction. For them, study and practical activities are an integrated whole. The part-time education system is in full accordance with basic socialist pedagogic principles, and it is a very effective way of bringing up the able revolutionary workers who are needed in socialist and communist society.

As almost all the part-time schools are attached to regular educational institutions and production enterprises, teachers, education facilities and proper conditions for experiments and practical training are readily available. Besides, the part-time system of education does not affect the manpower situation in socialist construction, for it enables the workers to study without halting their productive labour.

We should allow the study-while-you-work system to display its full superiority and develop it to meet the demands of the changing situation.

Now that universal 11-year education has been established, the working people's senior middle school will soon become unnecessary, and the system of higher education and regular study system of cadres and working people will in the future become the basic part-time education system. In order to offer higher education to all members of society in accordance with the Party's policy for making the whole society intellectual, it is necessary to continue to expand and improve the part-time system of higher education. In particular, factory colleges should be further expanded, the education there improved and farm colleges set up in the rural areas to give higher education to rural officials and agricultural workers.

4) THE STATE SYSTEM OF BRINGING UP AND EDUCATING CHILDREN

In order to bring up children to be masters of society and communist builders of the future, they should be raised and educated collectively in modern surroundings from early childhood. If children are brought up collectively, they become accustomed to an organizational and disciplined life and develop collectivist ideas and communist moral qualities from childhood, and this is a great help to their mental and physical development.

Our Party and the Government of the Republic have always devoted a great deal of effort to the work of bringing up children under public care. After liberation we set up nurseries and kindergartens in towns, at factories, enterprises and state farms and ran them at great cost to the state, and thus we established a system of bringing up and educating children under public care. Even in the difficult circumstances of the Fatherland Liberation War, bringing up children under public care was still continued, and such great measures as setting up large numbers of baby homes and orphanages and raising war orphans were adopted. After the foundations of an independent national economy had been laid and the socialist system established in the postwar years, the work of nursing and educating the children at state expense got under way in earnest. With the planned investment of state funds and through a movement that involved the whole of society, numerous modern nurseries and kindergartens were built throughout the town and country' areas and their management was systematically improved.

This led to the establishment in our country of a solid socialist system of nursing and educating children, under which all preschool children were brought up collectively at nurseries and kindergartens at state and public expense.

Our state system of bringing up and educating children is the most progressive of any such system, embodying the communist principles of child-rearing. Bringing up children collectively under public care is an important communist policy. Socialist and communist society is a society based on collectivism, and collective education is the basic form of training communists. Only by nursing and educating children collectively in social surroundings is it possible to bring them up to be people with truly communist qualities.

That the state and society bear the costs of nursing and educating children is also based on communist principles. In our country the children are educated and brought up at state and public expense, with the result that all the children are equally entitled to all state and social benefits, irrespective of their parents' occupations and the quantity and quality of their labour.

The state system of nursing and educating children should be consolidated and developed still further. The institutions for bringing up and educating children should be further modernized and managed properly, and the standard of nursing and educating children should be raised steadily on the basis of socialist pedagogy. In order to bring up and educate the children better and enable women to take part in public life, many weekly and monthly nurseries and kindergartens should be gradually established.

Supply services for the nurseries and kindergartens should be improved. A well-regulated state system of supply should be established and the foodstuffs, toys, teaching aids and furnishings, medicines and nursing facilities that are needed for bringing up and educating children should be supplied in sufficient quantities.

5. THE DUTY AND ROLE OF EDUCATIONAL INSTITUTIONS: GUIDANCE AND ASSISTANCE TO EDUCATION

Educational work in socialist society is an honourable and important revolutionary task assigned to the educational institutions and educationalists. In socialist society educational work is Party and state work and the concern of the whole of society. For socialist education to run smoothly, the functions of educational institutions and the part educational workers play should be enhanced and Party guidance, state support and social assistance in educational work should be carried out in full.

1) THE MISSION AND DUTY OF SCHOOLS

In socialist society, the school is the base for revolutionary training and the centre of the cultural revolution. Through its work the school contributes to the ideological and cultural revolutions. The mission of the school in socialist society is to help the younger generation grow up to be communist and produce cadres according to the fundamental principle of socialist pedagogy.

Bringing up the younger generation to be communist is a project for the everlasting prosperity of our country. The younger generation represents the future of our country and our children are heirs to the revolutionary cause. Ultimately, the future of the country and the revolution depends on how the younger generation is brought up.

Training cadres is a decisive factor in promoting the revolution and construction. It is they who will decide everything. Without cadres who are well prepared politically and ideologically, as well as technically and practically, we cannot solve the difficult problems that arise in building a new society, nor can we ensure a rapid development of the economy, culture, science and technology.

School should make an active contribution to the cause of socialism and communism by working efficiently to bring up the younger generation to be communist and to train cadres. In order to discharge its mission in full, the school must first organize and conduct education administration properly. A fundamental aspect of education administration is to ensure that the work of educating the students goes through precisely the required processes of pedagogy.

The first process of pedagogy is the preparation of the education programme. Organs of education administration and institutions of higher learning should draw up a good education programme based on the basic principles of socialist pedagogy and in conformity with the demands of our revolution and the actual situation in our country and with the development of the ideological consciousness of the people and the patterns of learning in science and engineering and put it into effect.

Education administration at the schools should give guidance to the teachers so that they make adequate preparations for teaching. The cardinal point in preparing to teach is to draw up a good plan. Education administration at the schools should always check the teachers' personal plans without fail and help them to complete them through collective discussion. When teaching new subjects and giving lectures on new matters, model lectures or demonstration lectures should always be arranged.

Education administration at the schools should guide the teachers so that they cover the whole education programme. The key problem in guiding teaching is to maintain both political and ideological principles and scientific accuracy. Education administration should see to it that the teachers establish *Juche* thoroughly in their instruction and base the lessons strictly on

Party policy and impart to the students working knowledge that will be useful for the revolution and construction. In addition, the latest scientific and technological breakthroughs should be introduced promptly to enrich the content of the lessons and to steadily raise academic levels.

Education administration should guide the teachers so that they improve their methods and use every teaching method that is envisaged in the schedule including lectures, discussions, experiments, practice and essay writing.

Education administration should regularly examine and take note of how much the students have digested of the subjects they have been taught and organize work for improving their academic performance.

Putting school work on a regular basis and managing it according to regulations is an important task of education administration. This means that educational work should be conducted in conformity with the requirements of scientifically-arranged pedagogical processes and that the revolutionary system and discipline should be established at school.

A scientific system of education administrative guidance should be established at the schools; education should be geared towards pedagogical requirements; and the whole work of the school education administration from the drawing up of educational plans to their implementation, should be organized and guided in a coordinated manner.

Strict discipline must be established in schools so that the education programme is carried out without fail. The proper execution of the education programme is a task assigned to the schools by law and the most important educational discipline. The school should establish the revolutionary discipline of implementing the education programme to the letter and without question and thoroughly carry out the curriculum and syllabuses.

Schools should guide the extracurricular activities and political and organizational life of the students in a responsible manner. In socialist society the school is entirely responsible for the education of the students. That is why the school should be responsible not only for teaching but also for the students' extracurricular activities and should organize and guide properly not only the students' studies but also their organizational life and social and political activities. Both the educational environment and the management at schools should be good.

A good educational environment and good management are important factors in discharging the mission and role of the school as the organ of ideological education and the base of the cultural revolution; they are also important in training the students to be good workers who are educated and enlightened enough to manage the economic life of the country carefully.

The educational environment at school should befit an organ of the ideological revolution and it must be conducive to learning; it should also contribute to cultivating Party loyalty in the students, to making them understand the correctness and vitality of Party policy and to increasing their revolutionary consciousness. Moreover, schools should be improved in such a way as to help the students to consolidate what they have learned and to understand the realities of the country.

The school should be built up as the base of the cultural revolution and should be managed carefully. In school, classrooms, study rooms, laboratories and all other facilities should be maintained spick and span, and a mass-based management system should be established so that all the teaching staff and students play the part of master in school management.

2) The Position and Role of Teachers

Teachers are in direct charge of educational work. In our society they are career revolutionaries who bring up the members of the younger generation as heirs to the revolution and as communists. The quality of the young people, heirs to the revolution and the future of the country, depends on how well the teachers fulfil their honourable mission. Teachers are responsible to the Party and the revolution for the future of the country.

The primary duty of a teacher is to teach well. Teaching is also his primary revolutionary duty. Teachers must teach the students well and, at the same time, guide them responsibly in their out-of-school studies and activities.

In order to educate the younger generation properly, teachers must themselves acquire revolutionary and working-class traits. Unless teachers acquire revolutionary and working-class qualities, they cannot imbue in their students revolutionary and working-class qualities; and unless they become communist themselves, they cannot train their students to be communists.

The basic way of making teachers into revolutionaries is to improve their activities in the political organizations. Teachers should take a more active part in Party and working people's organizations and in particular intensify criticism.

Teachers must steadily temper themselves through practical revolutionary activities. Teaching is their major practical activity. They should put all their talents and energies into education and, in the course of this, temper themselves politically and ideologically. They should go among the workers and farmers to conduct their social and political activities and spread scientific and technological knowledge among them while learning from them.

Teachers must steadily improve their qualifications. The qualifications of the teachers decide the quality of education. To teach well, teachers must not only be steadfast politically and ideologically but also have good scientific and theoretical qualifications. You must know ten times more than you teach.

Teachers must have a full understanding of both Party policy and their own specialty. They should also have some knowledge of a variety of other fields, including elementary science, be acquainted with domestic and international affairs, the situation in our country and educational theory and methods. University teachers must hold academic degrees in their subject, and teachers in general education should all be qualified.

In order to improve their qualifications, teachers must establish the revolutionary habit of study. All teachers must study regularly and hard and read a great deal. Organization and guidance must be strengthened in order to improve the teachers' qualifications. Model and demonstration lectures, scientific discussion and meetings to exchange experience with others should be conducted frequently, and state examinations held regularly to test and judge the qualifications of the teachers.

In order to bring up the students to be communist revolutionaries, the role of LSWY and CU instructors at school should be enhanced. LSWY and CU instructors at school must directly organize and guide the lives of the students and children in the LSWY and CU and train and protect them politically. They should also be responsible educators who guide the activities of students and pupils after school hours.

The role of nursery school and kindergarten teachers should be enhanced. Nursery school and kindergarten teachers bring up and educate children under social care. They should work in a communist way and prepare the little children for school.

Teacher training should be improved. A well-regulated system should be established to train teachers and priority given to teacher training. Teacher-training centres such as universities of education and teacher-training colleges are "breeding stations" for the education of the younger generation. It is only when teacher-training centres educate their students proficiently that they can produce excellent teachers who are prepared politically and ideologically, scientifically and technically; only then can all the children and students be brought up as able revolutionaries. Promising young men and women should be selected and admitted to universities of education and teacher-training colleges, and the level of teaching raised decisively there.

Teacher-training institutions must also pay close attention to training school LSWY and CU instructors and nursery and kindergarten teachers. Teachers on the job should attend frequent refresher courses. A system should be established to re-educate the teachers according to a plan so that their qualifications always match the needs at the times. Short courses should be run regularly, to ensure uniformity in teaching and to raise the quality of teaching steadily.

3) PARTY GUIDANCE IN EDUCATION

Strengthening Party guidance in education is a decisive guarantee for developing socialist education fully into a Party and working-class education and for solving all the problems that arise in educational work.

Party guidance in education is, in essence, guidance based on politics, political guidance. The central task of Party guidance in education is to fully apply the fundamental principles of socialist pedagogy in educational work and to control and guide educational work properly, so that the Party's education policy is implemented correctly.

Party organizations must control and guide education in schools in particular. The school is the basic unit of education. Party organizations must always keep themselves informed of the work of schools and guide them so that their education meets Party requirements and suits the interests of the revolution.

Party organizations must offer proper guidance to the organs of education administration. The Party's education policy is put into effect by these organs. Party organizations should guide them to play a greater part in implementing the Party's education policy and strengthening state guidance of education.

The teaching staff must be strengthened, and the work with teachers must be improved. Party organizations must reinforce the teaching staff with good people who stand steadfastly by the Party's monolithic ideology and adhere to a solid working-class position and hold high academic qualifications. There must be no one among the teachers who has not accepted the Party's monolithic ideological system.

Party organizations must exert tighter control over the political and organizational life of the teachers and work hard on their ideological education. In this way, they will guide all teachers to become revolutionary and working-class and to improve their academic qualifications and show great revolutionary enthusiasm and creative activity in educating the younger generation.

Work with the students must be done well. The main revolutionary task that students are given is to study. Party organizations should guide students to treat their studies as their primary revolutionary task and to work hard at them. A revolutionary habit of study must be established, particularly among university students. Thus, all of them will acquire a full knowledge of their speciality, master at least one foreign language and become fully qualified as cadres before they graduate.

Party organizations must give responsible guidance in the organizational and ideological life of the students and direct great efforts to their political education and organizational tempering. Party organizations must direct school LSWY and CU organizations to do their work satisfactorily. They should appoint good LSWY and CU instructors to the school and always educate them well. They must also see that LSWY organizations at all levels direct their main efforts towards working with schoolchildren and students, and must offer better guidance to school LSWY and CU organizations.

Party organizations must control the student enrolment at universities strictly in accordance with Party and working-class principles. Institutions of higher education must admit young people who have completed secondary education and have been tempered through work or in the army, are fully prepared ideologically to serve the Party and the revolution and are good at their studies.

In order to improve Party guidance in higher education, Party committees at universities must play a bigger part. Institutions of higher learning have large numbers of teachers and students who are Party members, and there are Party organizations at faculties and departments and among students. These institutions organize and carry out all kinds of education administration independently, starting with drawing up the education programme. Therefore, increasing the Party committees' role in the guidance of all their work is a major guarantee for being successful in higher education.

The principal task facing university Party committees is to establish the monolithic ideological system of the Party among the teachers and students and to train all the students to be able cadres and fine builders of communism, as required by the Party. These Party committees should organize the implementation of the Party's education policy responsibly and discuss every major university problem collectively, adopt sound measures and implement them. The Party committees must consolidate their own and the LSWY organizations at universities, increase their role and always control and guide the organizational and ideological life of the teachers and students.

4) STATE SUPPORT AND SOCIAL ASSISTANCE IN EDUCATION

The material needs of socialist education, which enables all members of society to study, are indeed enormous. Also, socialist education requires modern facilities. It is only when a state that is based on a strong independent socialist economy takes the responsibility to support education that the tremendous material needs of education can be met and modern facilities provided.

The state must steadily increase its investment in education and make adequate provision for educational needs. The state must give priority to building schools to cope with the increasing number of students and the requirements of the developing situation and build good school laboratories and practical training centres. It must also provide ample textbooks, school equipment, teaching aids and furniture, and continue to improve and modernize them. It should improve those centres that produce education equipment and send them supplies on a planned basis. The state must set up good social educational establishments. It must build many modern social educational establishments, including students and children's halls and CU camps.

In socialist society all members of society must play their part in education and the whole of society must offer active support. In socialist society all working people should be educators of the young and help in education.

The working people, who are the parents, should always guide and help their sons and daughters in their studies and become involved in the social education of all the children and young people.

We should launch a widespread campaign to mobilize the support of the whole of society in laying down material foundations for schools. All factories, other enterprises and cooperative farms should form supporters' organizations to give great manpower and material aid to the schools in the neighbourhood. Publishing houses, factories and other enterprises must send new books, machinery and equipment to the schools on a preferential basis, when these are needed for educational purposes.

* * *

It is the sacred and honourable revolutionary duty of communists to run education properly. For good education is an important guarantee for the victory of the revolution and promises a brilliant future for our prospering homeland. We should develop socialist education and take it to new heights on the basis of the successes already achieved in educational work.

We should train all the members of the younger generation

to be dependable builders of communism by educating them well, to make them fitting heirs to our revolution. We should bring about a turn in training our own officials to meet the demands of the developing situation and train more able people to serve the revolution and construction. We should establish the revolutionary habit of study across the nation and lead all the members of society to work while studying and study while working so that their cultural and technical attainments steadily improve.

Our Party's education policy has been tried and found to be correct beyond all doubt. We will carry through the *Theses on Socialist Education* which embodies the Party's education policy, and thus achieve still greater success in socialist education.

4

ON THE FULL IMPLEMENTATION OF THE *THESES ON SOCIALIST EDUCATION*

Kim Il-Sung

Editor's note: *This speech, delivered after the deliberation on, and eventual adoption of, the* Theses on Socialist Education, *concluded the 14th Plenary Meeting of the Fifth Central Committee of the Workers' Party of Korea, on September 7, 1977.*

COORDINATION BEGINNING WITH PRESCHOOL

The *Theses on Socialist Education,* published at this meeting, throws light both on current practices in education and on innovations that are to be introduced. I would like to make a few brief remarks on just some of the questions relating to its implementation.

First of all, we should coordinate preschool, school, and adult education. The *Theses on Socialist Education* makes a point of coordinating preschool, school, and adult education so that all the people receive education throughout their lives. In order to train every member of society to be of a communist type equipped with the revolutionary world outlook and with considerable scientific and technical knowledge, it is necessary to educate them all from childhood until the day they die.

Preschool education is the first stage of education. It plays a major role in forming a man's world outlook and has a great influence on his intellectual development.

In this country preschool education is provided in the main at kindergarten. Therefore, the work there should be improved to give a good upbringing to the children below school age.

In educating children below school age, those who remain at home without attending kindergarten pose a problem. Party organizations and educational institutions should study the question of educating these children and take appropriate steps.

Schooling is the basis of all education. Only when children and adolescents are properly trained during secondary and higher education can they be raised as communist revolutionaries equipped with a revolutionary world outlook and a full knowledge of science and technology. Therefore, we should increase the sense of responsibility and role of education workers so that they teach well.

Continuous Education:
Building Socialism from a Reactionary Culture

Education does not end after preschool and school education. Even after leaving school, people should still receive continuous education.

Adult education is as important as preschool and school education. Even after graduating from university and going out into society people should continue to receive education. Only then can they devote themselves wholeheartedly to fighting for the Party and the revolution whatever the adversity.

In my experience of working with tens of thousands of people from the time when I began the anti-Japanese revolutionary struggle to this day, nearly all of those who turned degenerate were people who neglected to study. If iron is left outdoors, it will rust and become useless. To prevent this, it must be oiled or painted.

Since we are building socialism against a capitalist background, bourgeois reactionary ideas and degenerate culture may infiltrate from outside and all sorts of outdated ideas, including feudal and capitalist ones, may exert a corrosive action domestically. If bourgeois reactionary ideas infiltrating from outside and outdated ideas remaining in the minds of the people are combined, their corrosive action will be still greater. Under such circumstances, if we do not intensify the education of the people to make them thoroughly revolutionary, they may fall prey to degeneracy.

If people dislike studying and hate life in an organization, they will become degenerate. Even some of those who participated in the anti-Japanese armed struggle became degenerate. They simply went hunting and fishing and did not study or participate in the organizational life of the Party. Even those who have been engaged in the revolutionary struggle for many years should continue to study and be loyal to their Party organizations. Only then will they avoid becoming degenerate and remain sound to the end of their lives and preserve the honor of a revolutionary fighter. Revolutionaries should be faithful to the Party and the leader, to the country and the people till the end of their days. Only then will they retain the respect of the people even after they have died.

A considerable number of university graduates have become corrupt because they did not study properly after going out into society. A man will not always acquire a correct world outlook just because he has graduated from university. At university only the basis of a revolutionary world outlook is laid. So, even after leaving university and becoming a full member of society, one must continue to study and develop one's revolutionary world outlook.

Historical experience shows that anyone who neglects studies and Party life will go astray, whether he is an old revolutionary fighter or a university graduate.

BUILDING THE IDEOLOGICAL FORTRESS OF COMMUNISM

The publication of the *Theses on Socialist Education* is aimed not only at educating the younger generation but also at capturing the ideological and material fortresses of communism through imbuing all the working people with revolutionary and working-class qualities.

We should improve adult education, so that all the working people consolidate and develop their revolutionary world outlook and steadily raise the level of their general knowledge and their levels of culture and skill.

In particular, careful attention should be paid to educating cadres. At present the revolutionary habit of study has not been properly established among the cadres. It is not the subordinates but the cadres who dislike studying. This is the case with cadres belonging to both central and local authorities; they seem to prefer just driving around in cars.

The cadres are now neglecting their Saturday studies on the pretext of meetings and other things. As I have always said, studying, too, is a revolutionary task. Therefore, you should attend these study sessions without fail, even if it means that you are unable to deal with some other work on Saturdays. The system of Saturday studies has now been well established, but the cadres do not keep to it faithfully.

Moreover, the system of month-long short courses is not being run properly. This was instituted after the 15th Plenary Meeting of the Fourth Central Committee of the Party, and it was made obligatory for all cadres to go to school for one month's study every year. For a few years after this system was established all the cadres without exception attended these courses, but now the courses are not being run regularly, and when they are given, they are restricted in scope. When told to attend, some chief secretaries of the provincial Party committees refuse, saying they cannot possibly do so at the height of the farming season. But as long as there are Party organizations, Party members and government bodies, farming in the province will not go particularly amiss because the provincial Party chief secretary is absent.

Without studying, the cadres cannot keep up with the developing situation nor play their role properly as the leadership personnel of the revolution.

By establishing the revolutionary habit of studying all cadres should become imbued with the revolutionary doctrine of our Party and acquire comprehensive scientific and technical knowledge.

Above all, they should study Party policy harder. It is only when they study Party policy closely that their political life can continue to flourish and they can advance bravely along the revolutionary road throughout their lives. Only then can they measure everything by the yardstick of Party policy, distinguish right from wrong and propagate its truth.

Since our cadres are failing to study Party policy properly, they do not propagate it well and when they are sent abroad, they fail to work without hesitation in conformity with its demands.

All cadres should study Party policy in depth, digest it thoroughly and use it as a strict basis for all their actions and their lives. Meanwhile, all cadres should have a complete understanding of their own work.

For this, they should acquire the latest scientific expertise. They should attend Saturday studies and Wednesday lectures without fail and go on the month-long courses with enthusiasm. If a whole month is too long, it could be shortened to 20 days or so, but the point is that the courses must still be run.

As far as studying is concerned, no exception can be made

for high-ranking officials. The members of the Political Committee of the Party Central Committee and officials of the Party Central Committee, Central People's Committee, Administration Council, economic establishments, educational and cultural institutions, and all other cadres should study. Under the slogan of "The Party, the people and the army must all study!" all cadres must persevere in their studies and in this way steadily improve their political-theoretical levels and their cultural and technical standards.

Next, the quality of education should be radically improved. This is an important, common concern of all the branches of education: primary, secondary, higher, general, and technological.

A "Working-Class Edge" to Teacher Training

Above all, we should bring about a marked improvement in the quality of primary and secondary education. This requires improving both the universities of education and teacher-training colleges. These universities and colleges are "breeding stations" for the education of the younger generation. They train teachers, so they can be compared to the breeding stations that hatch chicks; hence, in the *Theses on Socialist Education* I have called them "breeding stations" in simple language.

It is only when such "breeding stations" are improved and the standard of education raised that they can turn out many excellent teachers, and this will make it possible to improve the quality of primary and secondary education markedly.

If we do not train teachers efficiently, this will have serious consequences on educational work. Before the 15th Plenary Meeting of the Fourth Party Central Committee, education was in an extremely deplorable state. At the time there were many teachers and officials in the field who did not adhere to a firm working-class stand. As a result, they failed to give a sharp working-class edge to education and tended in the main to conduct education of a motley form and nebulous kind, on the borderline between working class and capitalist. At the time one particular teacher speaking from the platform at an education workers' congress preached bourgeois child psychology, saying that we should only teach young children such notions as red and blue, beautiful and ugly and not mix in political and ideological education, revolutionary education. And a leading official in the field of primary and secondary education applauded, rather than hitting out at him. Because the workers in the education field were in this state at the time, it was inevitable that they would be unable to give education a working-class edge, and instead they taught a motley form.

In our experience, people should be given revolutionary education from their childhood. During the anti-Japanese armed struggle, we gave revolutionary education to the members of the Children's Corps in the guerrilla zones. We taught them that the Japanese villains, landowners, and capitalists were our enemies and that they should learn from the People's Revolutionary Army and fight after their fashion in order to crush the Japanese, landowners and capitalists and build a decent society in our country. We even taught them how to beat the Japanese. Thus, these members of the Children's Corps grew up to become ardent revolutionaries.

If we fail to give a working-class edge to teaching and instead offer a motley education, people may become motley and not care who they earn their daily bread from—whether from the capitalists or the working class—and society may become a mixture of capitalism and socialism, neither one thing nor the other. Therefore, after the 15th Plenary Meeting of the Fourth Party Central Committee we concentrated great efforts on strengthening the ranks of education workers and giving a working-class edge to educational work.

Nowadays, all the foreigners who visit our country express great admiration for the excellent way in which we raise our younger generation.

One President who visited us a short time ago was greatly touched to see our children and young people lining his route to welcome him and performing the mass gymnastic display *Song of Korea*. In Korea, he said, the children and young people were very well educated: with a younger generation such as this, one need have no fear of anything. The strength of Korea is indeed invincible, he added. Then he asked me how we had brought them up and given them such organization and discipline to allow them to make such high ideological and artistic accomplishments. So I told him that it was essential to educate them properly and not give them a motley mixture of capitalism and socialism.

I have heard that in some countries now, if they are to mobilize people to welcome a foreign delegation, they have to give them a day's pay. Things will turn out like this if a motley education is offered with no working-class edge.

We should never rest content with the successes we have achieved in the field of education, but must continue to improve teacher training. Since the 15th Plenary Meeting of the Fourth Party Central Committee, I have taken every opportunity to stress the need to improve it.

However, the Science and Education Department of the Party Central Committee and the provincial Party committees have failed to take any decisive steps in this direction. The Party has placed the universities of education and teacher-training colleges entirely in the hands of the provincial Party committees, but none of the chief secretaries and secretaries in charge of education has ever given a lecture at these universities. Some officials plead a lack of knowledge for failing to deliver a lecture at the universities. But this does not stand to reason.

Party organizations should totally abandon the practice of ignoring teacher training and intensify their guidance of the universities of education and teacher-training colleges.

The provincial Party committees must reinforce the teaching

staffs at these universities and colleges and improve their ideological education and encourage them to take a more active part in the Party organizations, so that they teach in accordance with the requirements of the *Theses on Socialist Education.*

The provincial Party committees must provide these universities and colleges with ample laboratory and practical training facilities to improve teaching by means of visual aids and laboratory and practical training.

The proper combination of school and social education is very important in raising the quality of primary and secondary education. At present no deviation is evident in our social education. Good films are shown; TV broadcasts are wholesome; there is nothing decadent, like vulgar jazz dancing and loafing about, as in other countries.

But at present there is something wrong with the organization of the school children's' extracurricular activities. When they come home from school, they play football out in the streets or make mischief, because their parents are out at work.

The schoolchildren's extracurricular activities should be properly organized so as to stop them making mischief. To this end, it is necessary to build pleasant children's parks everywhere. If many children's parks are built and provided with various facilities, the pupils will be able to go and play there and carry on a variety of out-of-school activities. It would be a good idea to assign Children's Union instructors to these parks to guide the children's extracurricular activities.

Many libraries for schoolchildren should be built and run properly. Then, it will be possible to cultivate a love of reading in the pupils from childhood and thereby educate them.

At present, some personnel do not know how libraries should be managed, although it is not a very difficult task. In Pyongyang there are the Central Library and district and school libraries and all that is required is to run them properly. There is no need to build big, local libraries. Simply taking a few rooms of a house and installing books in them will serve the purpose.

In order to run the libraries well the state must provide them with plenty of books. However well a library may be built, if it has no books worth reading, the schoolchildren will not go there. Therefore, the state must publish a lot of books that will help in the education of the children and supply them to the libraries.

In order to run the libraries properly, it would also be a good idea to make pupils write synopses of the books they have read on a few sheets of paper and submit them together with the books when they return them to the libraries. This will put an end to the practice of returning books borrowed from the libraries without reading them and enable the children to learn how to write a composition. Where necessary, pupils' libraries and schoolchildren's halls must be built.

It is of greater benefit to use materials provided by the state to build pupils' libraries or schoolchildren's halls rather than noodle houses. It is no less important to build them than it is to build schools.

Many scientific films should be produced and shown to the schoolchildren and many science lectures given. A scientific film show will provide them with a lot of knowledge about science. It would be a good idea, when schoolchildren are assembled in the cinema, for a teacher, well-prepared for the occasion, to give a lecture on science for about 30 minutes before the film is shown.

EDUCATION IN THE CELLS OF SOCIETY

Good conditions should be provided for home education. The home is a cell of society and home education is a form of social education.

Yet, there is now a snag in home education. Parents are not educating their sons and daughters, not because they do not want to, but because of a lack of time. They come home from work so late at night that they have no chance to talk to their children.

Some working women are being compelled to do their job until eleven o'clock at night and to work even on Sundays. Some working mothers are even being mobilized in social efforts. Such being the case they have no time to look after their children and their homes.

In the future, sufficient time and proper conditions should be provided for parents to educate their sons and daughters.

On weekdays, except on Saturdays when they attend studies, the working women must be allowed to leave work unfailingly at seven or eight o'clock in the evening. In addition, the practice of mobilizing them for social work on Sundays must be totally eliminated, so that they can take care of their children at home and attend to their housekeeping properly.

Men should also be allowed to rest on Sundays. Those who are under the pressure of work can have a holiday in turn. On Sundays they should rest at home, educating their children, taking a walk with them, and attending to their own personal hygiene.

UNIVERSITY EDUCATION

The most important thing in raising the quality of education is to make a decisive improvement in the quality of higher education.

We are now striving to consolidate the material and technical foundations of the country and free the working people from difficult and arduous labour by fulfilling the three major tasks of the technical revolution as set out by the Fifth Party Congress. However, we are prevented from advancing forcefully in our efforts to implement these three major tasks because the qualifications of university graduates are low.

Many university graduates are incapable of managing the economy and ignorant of contemporary trends in scientific development.

Recently the Party Central Committee inspected Kim Chaek

University of Technology, the University of Construction and Building Materials and the Pyongyang University of Mechanical Engineering and found that they were in a deplorable state. Graduates from the University of Mechanical Engineering are unable to design a machine properly; they have not made an efficient machine.

Universities are not teaching welding properly, either. Nowadays welding is essential for both the machine industry and the construction industry. This is an age of welding, so to speak. But graduates from the University of Mechanical Engineering and the University of Construction and Building Materials do not know how to handle a welding machine, nor do they have a clear knowledge of welding-rods. That was why the machine and construction industries failed to bring about a revolutionary improvement in welding and retarded the fulfilment of the Six-Year Plan to a considerable degree. The graduates of universities of agriculture are not well qualified either.

Having directed agriculture myself since 1973, I have visited cooperative farms frequently, talking and listening to the farmers. I have also studied a lot of advanced farming methods which are being applied in other countries. In the course of this I have developed a farming method that suits our situation.

In our country agriculture is managed on scientific and technical principles in accordance with the Juche farming method. As a result, we harvest a very rich crop every year even under the severe influence of the cold front.

Until recently, however, universities of agriculture were teaching their students outdated farming methods, not the Juche farming method which we have developed.

Examples from Current Agriculutral Institutions

During my on-the-spot guidance tours of Kangwon and South Hamgyong Provinces last year, I investigated the situation in the rural economy and learned that the graduates from universities of agriculture had neither a clear idea of the *Juche* farming method nor a good understanding of world trends in agriculture. This led me to suspect that the universities of agriculture were not teaching their students properly, so I had the textbooks of the Wonsan University of Agriculture examined. The investigation showed that these textbooks contained quite a few theories that were contrary to our Party's Juche farming method. This farming method requires that crops should be planted closely, and that fertilizer should be applied at a number of different times to suit the biological characteristics of the crops. But one textbook in use at the Wonsan University of Agriculture said that close planting should be avoided because it would result in poor air circulation and that the whole amount of fertilizer for the rice crop should be applied by June 25.

When I was visiting North Hamgyong Province in the spring of 1976, I inquired into tobacco cultivation there. I learned that 12 tobacco plants had been planted per *phyong* and that the yield was barely one ton per hectare. This was too low a yield to permit us to supply the people with sufficient tobacco. Therefore, I told the officials in charge of agriculture in the province to ensure that tobacco was planted closely. Later I studied a variety of information on tobacco cultivation and discovered that in a foreign country a high yield of tobacco was being attained by sowing 30 plants or more per *phyong*. By contrast, the textbook used in our universities of agriculture said that more than 12 tobacco plants sown per *phyong* would cause poor air circulation.

No wonder that the agriculturists who have been educated with such textbooks at these universities are unable to manage agriculture by the Party's *Juche* farming method.

Past and Future Trends in Higher Education

The failure to improve the quality of higher education in

the past was due mainly to poor Party and state guidance and to the senior officials in this field not doing their job properly and failing to exert themselves to implement the Party's education policy.

On the occasion of the 30th anniversary of the establishment of Kim Il-Sung University, I addressed the university presidents and the teaching staff, stressing the importance of radically improving the quality of education. However, the senior officials in charge of education neither conveyed the speech to their subordinates nor did they make arrangements to implement the instructions I had given in this speech. These senior officials have idled away their time in their offices, instead of visiting the universities and giving them guidance.

Party organizations at all levels and the senior officials in the field of education should rectify the shortcomings in higher education as soon as possible and radically improve the quality of higher education.

In higher education it must be ensured that the students are carefully taught the latest breakthroughs in natural sciences. Without finding proper solutions to the scientific and technological problems that arise in the building of socialism through the development of natural sciences, we cannot develop the country's economy nor attain the three major tasks of the technical revolution. Unless we develop natural sciences, we cannot capture the material and technical fortress of communism. Therefore, the institutions of higher learning must teach natural science subjects properly.

In particular, efforts should be made to raise the standards in basic science subjects such as mathematics, physics, and biology. Meanwhile, the students should be made proficient in handling modern machinery and equipment, including automatic control systems, through good teaching in mechanical and automation engineering. Furthermore, full preparations should be made to introduce compulsory higher education.

Making Society Intellectual

We are now confronted with the extremely honourable yet difficult task of making the whole of society intellectual.

Making the whole of society intellectual is an inevitable requirement of socialist and communist construction. We must make every member of society an intellectual so as to eliminate any distinction between mental and physical labour and build a communist society. True, in order to build socialism and communism, the working class, having seized power, must transform society on its own pattern in all spheres–the economy, culture, ideology and morality. But communist society will not arrive simply because we have imbued all the members of society with working-class qualities.

As you all know, communist society is a highly developed, civilized society, the members of which will all work according to their abilities and be provided for according to their needs. Unless people in communist society have high standards of cultural and technological knowledge and morality, they are in no position to run a highly developed, communist society. So, we should work tirelessly to make the whole of society intellectual.

To do this we must provide universal higher education and turn everyone into a fully developed communist whose cultural and technological accomplishments are as high as those of a university graduate.

Higher education for all means that education in institutions of higher learning must be compulsory for every member of society. In other words, it means enforcing universal compulsory higher education.

In our country compulsory higher education is not something in the distant future. Because the country has not yet been reunified, we cannot put it into effect, but if only reunification was achieved it would be easy to enforce compulsory higher education. Even under the present circumstances, in which the country is divided, compulsory higher education is quite feasible as long as we have the Party and the government.

Introducing Compulsory Higher Education

Since we are the first to present the question of compulsory higher education, its introduction will no doubt involve a number of difficult and complex problems. Nevertheless, it should not be treated as a vague notion. When Marx evolved the theory of communism in the last century, people had only a vague idea that it was something that would happen in the distant future. However, afterwards Lenin overthrew the capitalist system in Russia and conducted the socialist revolution, and socialism is now being built in many countries.

When in 1956 we suggested introducing universal compulsory primary education in this country, some people had only a vague idea of what this was. But we introduced it and followed it with universal compulsory secondary education. We have now enforced universal compulsory eleven-year education. Compulsory higher education, too, is not something that will be introduced in the far-distant future. If we put a lot of work into it and show determination, we will be able to effect it in the near future.

While consolidating universal compulsory eleven-year education, we must prepare well for the introduction of compulsory higher education so as to bring that into effect at some future date.

Needless to say, with universal compulsory eleven-year education now lying heavy on our hands, it is hard to introduce compulsory higher education right at this moment. Therefore, it should be introduced gradually county by county and province by province.

Factories and Intellectual Life

It is essential to improve factory colleges, above all else. It is impossible to enforce compulsory higher education simply by expanding regular universities. As there is currently a manpower shortage, we cannot afford to expand the regular universities. So, we must improve the factory colleges to such an extent that everyone can study while they work.

If the factory colleges are to be improved and managed properly, the education programme should be well prepared and the teachers well qualified. Technicians in the factories and teachers at regular universities can be mobilized to teach at the factory colleges. When instruction in a social science subject is to be given at a factory college, a social science teacher can be invited from a regular university, and when a natural science subject is to be taught, a technician from the factory can give the lecture. If the provincial Party committees and administrative committees were to organize the work properly, the problem of providing teachers for the factory colleges could be solved easily.

At the same time as improving the factory colleges, we should set up a large number of higher specialized schools attached to the factories. In major industrial areas we must establish technical schools alongside senior middle schools so as to give the pupils technical education.

We have now built many automated factories, but the number of associate engineers and assistant engineers working there is low, so university engineering graduates are operating general automatic control panels.

If things were being done properly, such equipment would all be operated by skilled workers. In the future the colleges and higher technical schools should train a large number of skilled workers as well as associate and assistant engineers.

Socialist Education and the Korean Communist Revolution

In addition, the state's backing and social support for education must be strengthened. It is only by doing this and providing schools with laboratories and practical training centres and other educational facilities that we can educate the students in accordance with the principles of socialist pedagogy and bring them up as communist revolutionary workers equipped with working knowledge.

To strengthen state backing and social support for education, first of all, the attitude to education should be corrected. We must reunify our divided country as soon as possible and build a socialist and communist society where there is no exploitation and oppression and everyone is comfortably off. To do so, we should educate the younger generation well. We can say that the education of the younger generation is fundamental to deciding the destiny of the nation.

We are now raising 8,600,000 children and students at state expense, giving them free tuition. This is by no means a simple matter. But if we let difficulties frustrate our provision of free education, we will not be able to raise them properly. It is true that if we were to abandon free education and divert the money to the production of consumer goods, we would be able to improve the livelihood of the people a great deal. However, we must not simply spend money on the people's livelihood for the moment without taking into consideration the future prosperity of the country and the nation. Bringing up all the children and students properly is a very important job which paves the way for the prosperity of the country and the nation.

However, our officials now regard education as of secondary importance and show only half-hearted interest in giving state backing and social support to it. That is why the laboratories and practical training centres at institutions of higher education are poor.

The Party, with a view to improving the quality of higher education, has recently decided to use valuable foreign currency to import laboratory and practical training equipment for Kim

Il Sung University, Kim Chaek University of Technology, the University of Construction and Building Materials, Pyongyang University of Medicine, and Sariwon University of Agriculture, and the University of Science.

Simply by resolving to do so and getting down to work, we can provide schools with enough good laboratories and practical training centres, and other education facilities. As the economic foundations of our country are strong, it is not very difficult to equip schools in this way. If we call upon the working people to make and send to the schools such facilities as they need to educate the younger generation, the workers will provide motorcars, machine tools, and every type of machinery for practical training by conducting a campaign for increased production. It all depends on how our officials work to develop education.

Once I conducted underground revolutionary work in a farm village. There were two old men in the village. One was very poor and the other well-off. The one who was living in poverty made up his mind to have his children educated and worked hard to ensure that they were all educated. On the other hand, the well-to-do man simply made his children work, without thinking of sending them to school, although he could well afford it.

We did enforce compulsory primary education and then compulsory secondary education, but this was not because we had plenty of funds. We regarded the education of the younger generation as a question affecting the future of the nation and, although we were poor, we were determined to introduce compulsory education. But some countries have not introduced compulsory education because of the great expense.

All officials must hold a correct view of education and must not fail to provide the material foundations and other amenities for educational establishments of all levels up to universities.

We must take on the responsibility of catering to the material needs of central and local institutions of higher education. The state should take charge of those which are under central authority, and the provincial Party committees, provincial people's committees and provincial administrative committees should look after those in their own area. Of course, the state must provide the local universities with textbooks and such like. However, the provincial authorities should assume the responsibility for furnishing the local universities with facilities for laboratory and practical training and a good educational environment. In the provinces the support organizations for schools should be formed from industrial enterprises and cooperative farms, which must be held responsible for supplying the needs of the schools in their charge.

Industrial enterprises should make it a rule to send to the universities those machines and equipment they produce on an experimental basis. A long time ago I said that when a new type of machine was made, it should be supplied first to the universities. But now the officials are wont merely to boast about a new machine being made, and never think of offering it to a university.

In the future, industrial enterprises should send the machines and equipment they produce on an experimental basis to the schools so that they can use them in practical training.

The provincial people's assembly should place educational matters on the agenda of its meetings and solve promptly any problems that arise in educational work.

A nonpermanent committee should be set up under the Education Commission and meet regularly. This committee should be made up of not only officials of the Education Commission but also the senior officials of other commissions and ministries, as well as scientists. Its task should be to discuss questions relating to educational work, including state backing.

Next, the Party's guidance of education should be improved so as to implement the *Theses on Socialist Education*. This is indispensable for rectifying any shortcomings in educational work in good time and developing education in accordance with the requirements of the theses.

All Party organizations should devote themselves to the implementation of the theses, considering this to be an important objective. In order to improve Party guidance of education, the combined and joint operations of the organizational department, information and publicity department and education department of the Party should be efficiently organized. Socialist education is in essence the work of remoulding people and work with people to foster everyone as a communist revolutionary worker who is fully equipped with a revolutionary world view and considerable scientific and technical knowledge.

Guiding the Implementation of the *Theses*

Therefore, in order to ensure that the *Theses on Socialist Education* is implemented successfully, these departments of the Party should form a triad and take educational work firmly in hand and guide it. Since they deal directly with people, they should naturally conduct the combined and joint operations together as a triad when guiding educational work.

In particular, the chief secretaries of the provincial, city and county Party committees should not concentrate only on economic work but take educational work firmly in hand and make it a function of their committees. But at present they are showing no concern for education and leaving it entirely to the secretaries in charge of information work or education.

For the purpose of improving educational work, I have stressed many times that the members of the Political Committee of the Party Central Committee and all other leadership personnel of the Party should visit institutions of higher education to deliver lectures and to settle problems arising in education. However, nobody has ever done this properly.

The provincial, city, and county Party committees now have secretaries in charge of ideological and educational work, but they, too, are indifferent to education. Since the leading officials of the provincial, city and county Party committees pay no attention to education, Party policy fails to find its way into the educational institutions promptly and is not carried out effectively.

The chief secretaries of the provincial, city and county Party committees should regard education as an important aspect of Party work and improve their guidance of it. It is necessary to review the implementation of the *Theses on Socialist Education* properly.

All Party organizations should work all the time to develop in depth the work of implementing the theses.

It would be a good idea, as the current plenary meeting of the Party Central Committee has proposed unanimously, for the 5th of September, the anniversary of the publication of the *Theses on Socialist Education,* to be fixed as Education Day. Students' Day should be abolished, once Education Day has been instituted. Because this country is a "country of education" and a "country of learning" where everyone studies, there is no need for Education Day and Students' Day to be separate. You should not abolish the Anniversary of the Foundation of the Children's Union simply because Students' Day has been revoked. Since June 6, when the Children's Union was founded, is a historic day, this anniversary should be kept.

Even though Education Day has been instituted by this plenary meeting of the Party Central Committee, you should not simply observe it as just a holiday.

In celebrating Education Day every year, all Party organizations and educational institutions should make it a rule to review the work they have done to implement the *Theses on Socialist Education.* When Education Day comes round, the officials of all Party, government, administrative and economic organs and working people's organizations should review at a high political and ideological level the achievements and shortcomings in the year's efforts to implement the theses and take concrete measures to carry it through. And all officials should resolve to make the theses fully effective.

All Party organizations must see that the whole Party, all the people and the entire army study the *Theses on Socialist Education* in depth and digest it thoroughly. Only then can they discover ways of putting into practice the tasks that are set in it and carry them out one by one.

Not only the Party, administrative and economic bodies and educational institutions, but also the army should study the *Theses on Socialist Education.* The principles of socialist pedagogy are equally applicable to the People's Army. Without these principles soldiers cannot be trained as ardent revolutionaries, as communists. True, the technical subjects taught at universities may differ from those taught in the People's Army. But the principles of socialist pedagogy are the same.

The *Theses on Socialist Education* should be studied persistently over a long period of time rather than hurriedly. All Party organizations should see to it that it is studied tirelessly, step by step. An intensive study of the theses is particularly important for cadres; otherwise, they will be unable to implement it thoroughly.

After the *Theses on the Socialist Rural Question in Our Country* had been published, our officials did not study it carefully. So, the policies set out in the rural theses were not carried out properly. As the senior officials worked with no clear understanding of the main idea of the rural theses, they did not follow up the completion of the irrigation programme with the work to mechanize farming. In order to make rural mechanization a reality, they should have produced a large number of tractors and carried out land realignment, but they did not take any steps to do this.

Since the implementation of the *Theses on Socialist Education* involves training all members of society to be communist revolutionary workers, it is a more difficult and complex matter than carrying out the *Theses on the Socialist Rural Question in Our Country.* Therefore, all cadres should study the education theses even harder, gain a clear idea of its essence and make thorough ideological preparations for implementing it.

The *Theses on Socialist Education* is not an empty theory but a scientific theory that has been verified in practice. We advanced the idea of socialist education a long time ago and have accumulated rich experience and grown in conviction in the course of putting it into practice.

The *Theses on Socialist Education* contains many proposals which have either been translated into reality already in this country or are now being put into effect. So, if the entire Party, the whole country and all the people get down to work, the theses will be put into practice with success.

I hold the firm belief that with the full implementation of the *Theses on Socialist Education* you will develop education and take it onto a higher stage in keeping with the needs of the times.

AFTERWORD

CHONGRYON: THE STRUGGLE OF KOREANS IN JAPAN

Derek R. Ford

Editor's note: *This article was originally published on January 30, 2019 on LiberationSchool.org. It details the history of Koreans in Japan and the central role education played—and plays—in their fight against discrimination in Japan and for the peaceful reunification of their homeland.*

"The history of Chongryon is a history of unity, solidarity, and struggle."
–Chairman of the Yokosuka Chongryon Branch
Jan. 17, 2019

INTRODUCTION

In early 1956, construction was almost complete on what the Japanese authorities and general public thought was going to be a battery factory in what is now known as West Tokyo, but what at the time was farmland. When the "factory" was finished on April 10 of that year, however, a banner outside the perimeters announced that it was the new home of Korea University, which was previously a series of shacks attached to Tokyo First Korean

High School.

This episode is part of the much longer and widely unknown anti-colonial struggle of Koreans in Japan, a struggle with implications and lessons for the whole world. It's a struggle that, just like the Korean struggle more broadly, has been systematically isolated. As such, it's a struggle that needs more international solidarity, particularly from those of us in the U.S. Yet it's also a struggle that can provide hope and inspiration for all people fighting against colonialism and imperialism.

What's more, it's a struggle in which education—one of the foremost tasks of those interested in revolutionary transformation—is the motor.

Today there are around 800,000 Koreans living in Japan who are foreign nationals, or "special permanent residents" with either north or south Korean nationality. Japan is their home but, because of the U.S.-imposed division of Korea and the U.S. occupation of south Korea, they don't have their homeland back yet.

In Japan they face legal, political, and economic discrimination, and especially since 2002, have even suffered physical attacks at the hands of the Japanese authorities and right-wing groupings. Chongryon, or The General Association of Korean Residents in Japan, is the organization—or better, *movement*—fighting for the rights of Koreans in Japan, supporting their livelihood, maintaining their culture and language in the face of ongoing colonialism, and working for the peaceful reunification of their homeland.

THE ORIGINS OF KOREANS IN JAPAN

There are broadly three ways that Koreans came to Japan in the modern era, which together explain how a distinctive—yet by no means totally homogenous—Korean community came to reside in the colonial motherland. They also reveal the ways that

Japanese colonialism and U.S. imperialism created the Korean diaspora more broadly.

Primitive Accumulation

The Japanese conquest of Korea was a long process met with fierce resistance. It began in 1876, when Japan forced open Korea's trade ports and began expanding into Ganghwa Island in the West Sea of the peninsula. Through a series of political and legal steps—each backed up by force or the threat of force—Japan annexed Korea in 1905 and, in 1910, formally subjected the peninsula to colonial rule.

The Japanese colonization of Korea was, like all colonizations, brutal. Japan violently repressed Korean society, politics, and culture, outlawing all manner of political organizations as well as the Korean language. The Japanese even forced Koreans to take up Japanese names.

A growing industrial power, Japan required colonies for raw materials and, increasingly, cheap labor. With Europe embroiled in World War I, Japanese industrial manufacturing displaced European manufacturing, which led to an export-driven boom in the 1910s. With the expanding economy, workers were fighting for a bigger share of the profits. Between 1914 and 1919, the frequency and intensity of strikes rapidly grew and intensified. Japanese capital needed to break the power of organized labor by importing cheap labor.

At the same time, Japan was in the process of dividing up common lands in Korea through a nationwide land survey project. They ultimately redistributed lands from peasants to landlords via inflated prices and taxes, reassessing values, redrawing boundaries, and instituting a registration system. This is an example of what Marxists refer to as "primitive" or "primary" accumulation, the process by which capitalists acquire capital and produce the proletariat not through their ingenuity and frugality, but theft and violence. The land survey bankrupted small peasant farmers, transferring land to Japanese and a very small number of collaborating Korean landlords.

As they were driven off the land, Japanese companies worked with the colonial police to recruit workers to Japanese factories. There was widespread deception in this process. Workers were promised high-paying jobs and freedom of travel, but arrived to find the opposite. Many demanded repatriation, but companies rarely, if ever, obliged.

With the end of World War I, the Japanese economy went bust, beginning with the March 1920 stock market crash, the worst economic crisis up until that time. Even though Korean labor was cheaper and more contingent than Japanese labor, they were the first to be fired. For the next few decades, those who were lucky enough to find work were employed as day laborers in large-scale urbanization projects, working the most dangerous jobs for the lowest pay. It was Koreans who built many of the dams, roads, and housing projects that still exist in Japan today.

Sexual Slavery

The extensive Japanese sexual slavery network represents another aspect of the movement of Koreans to Japan. The Japanese military deceived and kidnapped hundreds of thousands of women to serve as sexual slaves to Japanese soldiers.

This practice couldn't have been more brutal. The women were systematically raped and beaten dozens of times a day. When they became too sick, they were killed or left to die alone.

While these so-called "Comfort Women" were kidnapped from Japanese colonies from Taiwan to the Philippines, most came from Korea and Manchuria (and a large percentage of people in Manchuria during this time were Korean).

The practice continued in the southern half of Korea after the Japanese empire collapsed in 1945 and the U.S. stepped in. In other words, when the U.S. took over control of Korea from Japan below the 38th parallel, they also took control of these rape stations. During the war against Korea, these stations served troops from the Republic of Korea as well as from the United Nations.

The struggle for justice for these women goes on and is an important part of the broader Korean peace and justice movement. So too does the repression of this struggle continue. The Japanese government has recently waged a campaign to get cities across the world to remove statues of and memorials to "Comfort Women" from San Francisco to Manila. They've even tried to influence U.S. textbook publishers to omit any mention of Japanese sexual slavery. Although all but a few dozen have already died, their spirit still pushes the Korean struggle forward.

Political unrest reverberated throughout these decades, as economic depression merged with anti-colonial demands. March 1, 1919 saw the launch of a massive Korean independence protest movement.

Two years before, the Bolshevik Revolution gave new form to the Korean struggle for liberation. Communists and anarchists began meeting in the borderlands of Russia, China, and Korea. In the early 1920s, a series of Korean radical labor unions were set up in Japan. In 1925, 12 of these unions merged into Roso, which by the next year had a membership over 9,000, and another 3 years later a membership of over 30,000. In response, Koreans were severely repressed in Japan, with their movements policed and highly regulated.

Forced Labor

Despite the threat that the organized Korean population posed to interwar Japan, the Pacific War (World War II) brought the need for additional labor once more. With Japanese imperial ambitions mobilizing large segments of the Japanese adult male population, Japan brought upwards of 1 million Korean workers to make up for the labor shortages. They utilized the National Mobilization Law—passed in 1938 to get the empire into gear for war—to forcibly conscript Korean workers and bring them to Japan, where they served as slave laborers. In some cases they were kidnapped from Korea, while in others they were deceived into coming to Japan for a brighter future. Once there, they had no control over their working and living conditions.

Working in munitions factories, construction, and mining, they also built secret underground bases to serve as plane storage and bunkers for the air force. Koreans, often children, built hundreds of thousands of miles of networks of tunnels with their hands and pick axes. Just before Japan's defeat in 1945, the government ordered all documents related to the project to be burned, so no one knows how many died in the construction. For the last several decades, Japanese and Korean activists have been studying this issue. Scholars have discovered that the tunnels were used to store munitions during the U.S. war against Korea.

Many of these slave laborers perished in the atomic bombings of Hiroshima and Nagasaki. They are never acknowledged in Japanese history.

A Chongryon Buddhist Temple, together with civic groups in Japan and both Koreas, have found some of the remains, and are currently working to bring them to the DMZ Peace Park.

The Collapse of the Japanese Empire in Korea: Defeat and Partial Liberation

Japan's unconditional surrender on August 15, 1945 didn't directly equate to the liberation of Korea.

Since 1931, nationalist and communist guerrillas struggled in the mountains of Manchuria against the Japanese. Kim Il-Sung emerged as a particularly effective leader during this period, so much so that the Japanese had special detachments tasked with his assassination. As the guerrillas were sweeping through Manchuria and the northern part of Korea, the U.S. moved to ensure that they wouldn't take the whole peninsula.

The night before Japan's surrender, two junior U.S. officers, Dean Rusk and Charles Bonesteel, took a National Geographic map of Korea into a room. Neither had been to Korea or spoke a word of the language. They divided the country along the 38th parallel, which was roughly in the middle but allowed the U.S. to retain control of the capital, Seoul. The U.S. and Soviet Union had already agreed to temporarily divide the country in half, with each army occupying the respective territory. The division was to last up to five years, by which point both Soviet and U.S. troops would leave.

With Japan's defeat, people's committees sprung up spontaneously all across the Korean peninsula. In the north, these would form the basis of a provisional government, and the Soviet Union would more or less rubber stamp all decisions made by this indigenous power. In the south, by contrast, the U.S. set up a military dictatorship, flying in Syngman Rhee, who had been studying in Princeton and Harvard and hobnobbing with the U.S. political establishment for decades. The dictatorship violently suppressed the people's committees and massacred the left.

It was evident to any observer that without U.S. military occupation, the nationalists and communists would win in Korea. As such, the U.S. moved to make the occupation permanent by holding elections in the south in 1948. Most of the population boycotted the election and the Soviet Union and provisional government in the north denounced the move.

In response to this artificial construction of the south Korean state, the Republic of Korea, the Democratic People's Republic of Korea was established in the north on September 9, 1948.

This served to heighten uncertainty and sharpen the struggle. Korea had been a united country for centuries and no one accepted the division into two states as legitimate or permanent. There is a general consensus that had the U.S. followed through with its initial agreement with the Soviet Union and allowed country-wide elections to take place, Kim Il-Sung would have won hands down. The U.S. certainly knew this, which again is why they created the south Korean state.

Koreans in Japan in an Uncertain Decade

By Japan's defeat on August 15, 1945, there were between 2 and 2.5 million Koreans living in Japan. A government survey found that 80 percent of Koreans in Japan hoped to return home, but they were unable to for three reasons. First, the General Headquarters—the U.S. overseer commanded by Douglas MacArthur—wouldn't let them bring any property with them. Second, those who did leave would not be allowed to return and visit their family that stayed. Finally, because Koreans had suffered under super-exploitation for decades, most did not have the means to repatriate.

Koreans in Japan were in a state of limbo. They, too, refused to accept the situation as legitimate or permanent. What's more, around 90 percent hailed from the southern half of the peninsula. Some did return home to find a U.S. occupation, violence, chaos, disease, and extreme economic insecurity. In fact, communists in the southernmost part of the country—who were geographically closer to Japan than the DPRK—fled to Japan to escape the military repression of the Rhee dictatorship in South Korea.

For example, 40,000 Koreans went to Japan after the South Korean authorities, backed by the U.S. military administration, smashed a nationalist and communist uprising on Jeju Island in 1948-1949. At one point 4/5 of the island's population lived in Osaka.

On October 15, 1945 nationalist, communist, and generally progressive Koreans in Japan formed *Joryon*, or the Federation of Koreans in Japan. *Joryon* increasingly looked to the provincial government in the north, and particularly the leadership of Kim Il-Sung, who was held in high esteem not just among Koreans, but also among Japanese radicals and intellectuals, and all progressive people of the world. *Joryon* thus had an alliance with the Japanese Communist Party (and indeed there was a long and complex history of cooperation between Korean and Japanese revolutionaries).

Education was the top priority for Joryon. Within a year there were hundreds of schools built with over 1000 teachers and 41,000 students. They made their own curriculum and published their own textbooks. They taught Korean history, language, dance, music, and politics.

The schools were set up to reclaim the Korean culture that Japan worked so hard to repress. It was also seen as preparation for an eventual return to a united Korea. The Japanese would later (and temporarily) embrace the repatriation efforts of Koreans to the DPRK out of a desire to get rid of the population they saw as "rebellious" and "ethnically inferior." Before the repatriation ended in 1984, over 90,000 had returned to the DPRK. Many sent some family members in the hopes that Korea would soon be reunited. As a result, many Koreans in Japan today have relatives in the DPRK.

The Joryon schools represented a threat to the post-war order and many were shuttered in 1946-7. Then, coinciding with the formation of the DPRK and RoK, in 1948-49 the General Headquarters violently raided and disbanded *Joryon* and its schools, killing several students in the process.

Mindan (The Korean Residents Union in Japan), a pro-US & Japanese rival organization, formed in 1946. Mindan was—and still is—loyal to the Republic of Korea, and Mindan members are south Korean citizens. They have not suffered any state repression, although members have still faced anti-Korean racism and discrimination.

Chongryon: Fighting Discrimination and for Peaceful Reunification

The U.S. war against Korea from June 1950 through July 1953 deeply entrenched the division of the peninsula. Koreans in Japan had to, in some sense, choose between the DPRK and the RoK. The overwhelming majority (around 90 percent) supported the DPRK, viewing it—instead of the U.S. puppet RoK—as the bearer of the Korean nation. After all, a popular and indigenous government ruled in the north, backed by the international prestige of Kim Il-Sung and other leading guerrilla fighters.

Under Japanese colonial rule, Koreans were Japanese nationals. But in 1952, their nationality was revoked. They lost voting rights, couldn't travel, and were excluded from a range of employment opportunities. They were stranded. Moreover, many were now second generation, meaning that they had grown up and lived their whole lives in Japan.

There were no Japanese schools where anything Korean was taught or even where students could speak Korean. Anti-Korean racism was rampant throughout Japanese schools and society.

A new organization for progressive, communist, and nationalist Koreans in Japan was in the works since Joryon's violent dissolution, but it wasn't until the early part of 1955 that a new organization, Chongryon, came into being. It was officially founded on May 25 of that year. The organization was founded specifically to organize Koreans in Japan around the DPRK, which meant working for peaceful reunification and creating their own educational and cultural institutions in Japan.

Chongryon looked inward to its own community and outward to its homeland. It thus took a position of non-interference in Japanese politics, adhering to Japanese laws (and thus severing ties with the Japanese Communist Party).

With generous funding from the DPRK—all the more significant given that the DPRK was at the time rebuilding its infrastructure after the devastation of the war—Chongryon set about rebuilding hundreds of schools as well as associations, sports teams, and professional and cultural institutions. They even set up their own bank and insurance company.

It was in this setting that Koreans in Japan built the "battery factory," or Korea University—the only Chongryon institute of higher learning.

Korean Education in Japan Today

Chongryon schools are relatively autonomous from Japanese control because they aren't technically "schools." Instead, under Japan's School Education Act, they are considered "miscellaneous schools." This means that they have their own curriculum but that they are self-funded, primarily through donations and tuition.

The schools are widely popular within the Chongryon community, but even Koreans in Japan who aren't affiliated with Chongryon send their children to the schools so they can learn their own language, culture, and heritage, and learn in schools free of anti-Korean racism. This is particularly so with elementary and middle schools.

There are currently 10,000 students in Chongryon primary and secondary schools. The composition is varied: around 45 percent hold DPRK passports, 55 percent hold RoK passports, and the remainder hold Japanese passports. Yet this doesn't mean that 45 percent support the DPRK, 55 percent support the RoK, and 10 percent support Japan. Being a DPRK foreign national carries an extra burden. They aren't able to freely travel outside the country, are prevented from visiting south Korea, and face increased discrimination. Many obtain RoK passports but still support the DPRK. This allows them to travel to both north and south Korea, as well as other countries like the U.S. and Britain. Holding an RoK or Japanese passport isn't a barrier to formal or informal Chongryon membership.

The autonomy of Chongryon schools comes at significant costs. Employers discriminate against those who hold degrees from Chongryon schools. Additionally, Japanese universities do not accept Chongryon degrees, and so students must pay for and pass an additional entrance examination.

In 2010, the Japanese government introduced a tuition waiver program for foreign nationals attending school in Japan. Students in Chinese and American schools, for example, have their education fully or highly subsidized by the government. The only schools excluded are Chongryon schools. This was *de jure* until 2013, when the Abe government made it official by revising a ministry ordinance. The official reason is that the government hasn't been able to verify Chongryon's curriculum (as the study was cut short by the Abe government). However, the government hasn't asked to verify the curriculum of *any* other foreign school.

Local governments, however, sometimes provide subsidies for Chongryon schools. Most, however, have followed the national government's lead and stripped subsidies.

Parents are also ineligible for tax exemption for donations made to Chongryon schools, unlike donations to all other foreign schools.

Such financial strangling tightens the noose around all of Chongryon and, by extension, the entire community of Koreans in Japan. With the Chongryon community excluded from so many sectors of the Japanese economy, parents aren't able to make up the difference through tuition, which means operating budgets and student enrollment decrease.

At Tokyo First Korean High School, where fourth and fifth

generation Korean students are taught by third generation Korean teachers, the operating budget is ¥2 million a year. Ninety percent comes from tuition and there is no government funding. Japanese high schools in the area get 50 percent of their funding from the Tokyo metropolitan government. The national government gives parents a ¥112,000 voucher, which covers tuition. Korean schools are the only schools ineligible for the voucher program.

Fed by the right-wing Abe government and its institutional attacks on the Chongryon community, racist and ultra-nationalist reactionaries have taken aim particularly at the most vulnerable: young students. In just one example, in 2009, 11 racists went to the front gate of a Chongryon elementary school in Kyoto and screamed things like "Cockroach Koreans!" at the students. After rallying for an hour, they proceeded to trash the soccer field and school auditorium. The group made three appearances at the school. The police showed up each time, but only stood by in silence.

A survey at a Chongryon middle and secondary school in Tokyo found that about 20 percent of students were harassed or threatened by right-wingers between 2003-2007.

Right-wingers have even attacked students with knives. Korea University students, for example, no longer wear traditional dresses outside of campus, because right-wingers slit their dresses with knives on the subway.

Throughout 2013, Japanese police conducted several raids on Chongryon. In February 2013, Japanese authorities raided Chongryon, deploying 250 police in more than 25 armored vehicles. Recently, a group of Korea University students returning from a school trip to the DPRK had all of their souvenirs confiscated at the Tokyo Haneda airport upon their return. The government has previously banned Chongryon officials from visiting the DPRK.

The Abe government regularly uses Korean students to try

and gain leverage in negotiations with the DPRK. This is an attempt to divide Koreans in Japan from the DPRK, which warmly hosts Korea University students and Chongryon members on a regular basis, and maintains close ties to the Korean community there.

The Human Rights Association for Korean Residents in Japan is involved in legal battles against this apartheid system. They regularly appeal to the United Nations Human Rights Commission.

The Future of Chongryon

After I first toured a Chongryon middle school in 2016, I met with the principal and vice-principle of the school. They asked us each our impressions. I was part of a delegation of overseas Koreans there to commemorate the 60th anniversary of the founding of Korea University, and I was the only U.S. citizen. When my turn came, I thought I would compare my observations with the state of U.S. schools.

I began by telling the administrators that, in the U.S., many people compare schools to prisons. At this point, my friend and colleague who was serving as my translator stopped, looking at me with a puzzled expression. After a few moments, another friend stepped in to translate. Afterwards, my colleague, who grew up in Chongryon schools and teaches at Korea University, apologized and explained what had happened. "I wasn't able to put what you said into words because it was such an alien notion," he said. "I couldn't even comprehend what you had said in my head, even though I knew all of the words."

Chongryon schools are joyous environments where students learn to be proud of their identity and their nation. In addition to learning Japanese language, history, and literature, they study Korean culture, history, and politics. They eat Korean food in the lunchroom. They study contemporary Korean politics carefully and closely. They have rock bands that write, produce, and perform their own songs about the reunification of their homeland. Chongryon schools accept *all* Korean students. There are no entrance exams and no one is turned away. The Chongryon Teacher's Union regularly meets to study what's known in the West as differentiated pedagogy (how to teach to each unique individual student).

It's no surprise that my colleague was so puzzled that he couldn't translate my remarks. Chongryon schools are the exact opposite of prisons. They serve as exemplars of the beauty and depth of the Korean yearning for peace and reunification. They provide educators and educational activists with a model of what genuine liberatory and decolonizing education can be. What if all oppressed people in the U.S. had schools where they had total control over curriculum and pedagogy?

The Chongryon movement deserves solidarity from all over the world, but particularly from those of us in the U.S. It is the U.S. government that is the main obstacle to achieving peace and reunification on the Korean peninsula. The constant demonization and propaganda against the DPRK is a fundamental obstacle to a mass pro-Korean peace movement in the U.S. Telling the story of the Chongryon movement is one way we can work against this propaganda and stand in solidarity with Koreans in Japan and Koreans everywhere.

The author would like to thank his friends in Chongryon and at Korea University for their help with researching and editing this article.

AFTERWORD